CARRY YOUR OWN BACKPACK

Carry Your Own Backpack

Simple Tools to Help You
Live Peacefully

Holly A. Schneider, LCSW

HOUNDSTOOTH
PRESS

CARRY YOUR OWN BACKPACK
Simple Tools to Help You Live Peacefully

ISBN 978-1-5445-2213-5 *Hardcover*
      978-1-5445-2211-1 *Paperback*
      978-1-5445-2212-8 *Ebook*

I dedicate this book to my husband and daughters, who by their mere presence in my life healed my heart. I wish for them to live by this philosophy, being clear about what belongs to God, others, and themselves. Each of you has brought a unique unconditional love to my journey. I couldn't carry my backpack without you. I accept the unique backpack that you wear securely. There is nothing sweeter than walking next to you, carrying our backpacks through life together.

CONTENTS

———

PREFACE 11

THE BACKPACK 15

MY BACKPACK 59

YOUR BACKPACK 79

THE BACKPACKS OF OTHERS 129

GOD'S BACKPACK.................................... 143

THE BACKPACK TOOLKIT 155

CARRYING OUR BACKPACKS TOGETHER 195

ACKNOWLEDGMENTS.. 201

RECOMMENDED READING LIST 205

When you know what belongs to you and what doesn't, your life changes forever.

Join me and the many who carry their own backpack. Walk next to us as you carry yours.

PREFACE

I am Holly.

I have been a psychotherapist for much of my adult life. Therapy is my true calling. I can't explain it. It has been my art, my fascination, my love, and my life's purpose. I knew when I was in college that my career would be about helping others understand their lives and manage their relationships. I have seen trauma impact many, walking beside them through the healing process. Coaching a wounded heart is an honored experience this side of Heaven. It is an intimate walk.

I began this love in my twenties while working on an inpatient behavioral health unit, treating adults and adolescents. I helped many in acute mental health emergencies that led to hospitalization. My clinical voice was nurtured while providing in-home family therapy, then transitioning to Christian adolescent residential treatment. Finally, I spent over thirteen years managing an extensive outpatient clinical practice. I was privileged to work with children, adolescents, adults, couples, families, and groups receiving treatment for mental illness. I would have remained in my clinical practice until retirement, but God had an adventure for me that I hadn't considered in my life's plan. I met the CEO of an innovative company who changed my life. He brought me into his fast-growing company to provide mental health services as a part of the workday, testing his wellness theory that, if people are happier at home, they are happier at work. By skillfully navigating well-being, employees work harder and grow into their purpose. Although this is strange to verbalize, I get a crazy surge of energy from sharing clinical tools with my clients to manage their difficult thoughts and emotions. I love watching people develop further in emotional intelligence, learning to be the best version of self.

Pain has been my friend, my teacher, my guide. I have spent endless hours reading, listening, and researching topics in wellness to help my clients move through trauma, understanding their needs and improving relationships. I adore helping people figure out their story. Every person's story matters.

I had my own story of pain and fear that led me to understanding mental health on a profound level. We all resist pain. I do too. It's easier to give others your happy self than it is to give them the truth. When we learn to embrace our full story, it becomes our greatest teacher. When we lean into our wounds with the purpose of healing, we stop judging ourselves and others. The stories about why we hurt can shift us from blame to resilience. This journey, in both helping others and understanding my own experience, brought me to a philosophy that changed my boundaries. I see it changing the lives of those I work with in my current role as an organizational life coach. I believe it will help you too. It is the story of the backpack. Once you apply this in your life, you will never be the same.

As I share my story, unpacking my backpack, you can do the same. As you learn to take the heavy items out of your backpack, your experience becomes lighter, which makes the hike more enjoyable.

I didn't know when I was young how important understanding myself would be. Honestly, we can't know what we don't know until we know it. I believe all things happen for a reason. The people who have hurt me didn't know how to do things better at the time. Pain has taught me well and made me conscious of how to love others, giving me gifts.

Similarly, the mistakes I have made were not on purpose. Each day that passes, I can do better. I consciously work at enhancing my well-being, a lifetime goal. I do this out of love for the unique experience I have been given, knowing that this world is temporary.

The losses in my life help me honor those around me who walk difficult paths. I don't wish my life to be different or better. From a heart of gratitude, I see the hand of God in all seasons of my experience. The pain that I have carried is nothing compared to that of my Lord. As a result, I journey through challenges sharing what I know to His glory.

I believe my parents did the best that they could to give me what I needed. I honor them despite hurts that came from not always being protected. We don't get everything we want. When we want what we have, it makes life easier. I want what I have. I let go of hurt, hanging onto beautiful moments that came from special people who loved me dearly. My losses, my blessings, and my experiences have made up the backpack I carry. Healthy boundaries helped me pivot from self-pity to peace and joy.

I have witnessed alcoholism, being affected by its hurts.

I have seen the terror of physical, emotional, and sexual abuse on its victims.

I have watched love abandon relationships, being replaced by hurt, lies, and revenge.

I lost people special to me and this ache will never go away, fully.

I had less childhood and more adulthood, but I rejoice in what it taught me.

My life could have been cut short by illness and injury, but it wasn't. That is not a mistake.

Resilience is my friend. No matter what, I bounce back. You can too.

My tools will make the difference!

THE BACKPACK

"It's not the load that weighs you down, it's the way you carry it."

—C.S. LEWIS

Choose to be happy. Decide to have peace with your past, live in your present, and create a better future. Focus on what belongs to you. Your backpack is the experience that belongs to you. It encompasses your thoughts, feelings, perceptions, goals, needs, values, standards, and choices. Carry your backpack. Let others carry theirs.

WHAT WE CARRY BUILDS STRENGTH

"Do not judge me by my success, judge me by how many times I fell down and got back up again."

—NELSON MANDELA

The first time I was drunk I was seven years old. My grandfather poured unlimited shot glasses of beer for me to drink at my infant sister's baptism celebration until I became sick. I remember my mother holding me in my bedroom. She was crying as I threw up. Her guilt was terrible. I was an innocent child, unnoticed until ill. Alcohol was a poison not managed properly in my family. I watched this poison change the personalities of family members, creating irrational fears, which reside within me. The day-old smell of alcohol on a body still makes me cringe, flooding my body with adrenaline. It is a smell you just can't get rid of in your mind.

I have preschool memories with my sister and cousin sitting unattended in the back of my grandfather's car, while he got drunk at a local bar. Grandpa was supposed to be caring for us. Instead, he was slamming drink after drink, leaving his innocent grandchildren alone in the car. When he returned, he would dangerously drive us home, swerving and passing cars with a wrath that triggered my panic. I would hold my sister's hand and lay on the floor behind the passenger seat to avoid throwing up. My sister had to protect me. She wouldn't let anything happen to me. This job helped her avoid her own fear. I blocked many of my childhood memories; it was easier than the reality of not being protected.

I learned early who you can trust and who you shouldn't. This is a useful skill when you are young. It shapes clear emotional instincts. This intuition from my backpack also has a negative side. It led to fear patterns that prevented me from asking for help, addressing difficult situations, and standing up for myself. As I unpack these experiences from my backpack, I can see how each negative event brought strength that led to insight and resilience, as well as a need for growth.

By nine years old I was working more than most teenagers and young adults. I had a wad of money in my piggy bank with stashes in various places, hoarding it. I often persuaded my older sister to buy things for me so I could save my money just in case of emergency. By twelve years old, I was working weekends for cash at a local bar my father managed. I spent endless hours in an environment not suited for children, as my parents worked to support us. Hard work became the thing I could control. I could please others because I was obedient. I could anticipate what needed to be done, working diligently with a great attitude. I had a constant stream of well-earned cash from old-fashioned hard work. While my friends all joined sports teams, I worked. This hard work became my control. I was good at it. It pleased those around me. It drove my need for a better life.

At thirteen I almost died from meningitis. Amy, my older sister, saved me. My mother was at work while I laid in the corner of our family room for hours in excruciating pain. I had lost vision from intense head and neck pain. It felt like my head was being crushed in a vice. Crying in agony, I recall hitting my head against the wall and even hallucinating. Amy was sitting with me, holding my fever-ridden head. I remember Amy begging my mother to return home in fear that I would die. My mother called her a "drama queen" for bothering her at work, but with pleading, she returned home. By the time I entered the hospital emergency room, I was limp and incoherent. I had grown used to the pain and didn't have the energy to fight it anymore. When the doctor quickly performed an emergency spinal tap, I have a memory of my mother draped over my body insisting she thought it was just a migraine.

Mom's ability to assess crisis was impaired from the normalized chaos that she lived in at the hands of her own parents. I knew that my mother had so much unresolved hurt in her heart that I learned not to make emotional waves, protecting her from additional struggle. Unfortunately, this left me alone to deal with my hurts. I would put on a smile and brighten the room no matter what was happening around me. Once stabilized, the hospital staff allowed my sister to visit me despite my quarantine. Amy was gowned in protective gear from head to toe. I thanked her for saving my life. She earnestly watched out for me in my youth. I depended on her emotionally for many years after that.

In school, I fought off bullies. I remember one boy who would target me and chant, "I would rather be dead than have red on my head." When he spotted me on the school bus, he would point and sing, creating laughter around him. I stood out with my bright red hair, dressed like a ragamuffin. I would avoid eye contact and act like it didn't matter. But it did. I had other peers in middle school and high school who commented negatively about my appearance. Mean words hurt no matter what age you are. This desire to be noticed for good became a driving force in how hard I pushed myself to succeed.

For much of my early adult life I fought off family drama with toxic relationships until I could stick to the boundaries that led to inner peace. I had family members who shouted ignorant opinions, fighting to get their way at the expense of others around them. I witnessed hostile conflict that was filled with lies and hate. Slowly I created distance with pushy, hurtful relatives who repeatedly challenged my limits. Having a family of my own made it easier to do that. I learned that, over time, people will accept your boundaries if you are consistent with them. The struggle with unhealthy family members motivated me to understand my own boundaries and hold my ground consistently. I would not repeat these learned patterns. I needed to be well inside.

A few years ago, my husband and I sat at our kitchen table with a dear friend. He had been through so much pain as a result of his divorce. He was one of the kindest people God had placed in my life. I told him that I was planning on writing a book. Smiling, he chuckled and said, "You certainly have the material, don't you?" Little did I know that only one month later, my friend would no longer be alive. Suffering from debilitating health issues, he passed during the night unexpectedly at the age of forty-eight. Following his death, I sunk into a sadness I hadn't known before. He loved others deeply, scattering joy to so many. He was a brother to me and was now gone. Loss changes our perspective. He was a teacher of unconditional Christian love, faithfulness, and dedication despite difficult circumstances. I write this, honoring what he taught me by example. The deep sadness from this loss validated the importance of living by consistent action, rather than just words. As my pain helped me unpack this lesson, I learned alignment from my values to live regardless of the hardship. It takes so much patience and peace to do that, especially in difficult circumstances.

Every road defined the emotional strength I needed to walk and teach the path of resilience. My story is uniquely mine. I am certain you also have an unparalleled narrative. Taking time to embrace your story is what the backpack journey is all about. Through the hills and valleys, it all matters.

I carry a backpack and so do you. This backpack holds our perspective, based on our story. Our thoughts and feelings come from *our* experience. Understanding and exploring brings insight. Our boundaries over time often become unclear because of emotions and thoughts that challenge us. We can have skills and tools in our backpack that help us understand our experience. This understanding helps us set necessary boundaries, which promote secure attachments. Healthy boundaries diminish self-doubt and provide emotional security. When we take time to understand our backpack, we develop insight into why we do what we do. Likewise, when we become peacefully curious about the backpacks of others, we create connection. I share my story with you to help you learn how to unpack yours for the benefit of insight and outsight. My toolbox can be useful in retraining insecure connections that come from your past. Understanding *you* is the key to understanding others who walk beside you. Thank you for joining me on this backpack adventure. I am grateful to be on this hike with you.

THE BACKPACK PHENOMENON

"God grant me the serenity to accept the things I cannot change; the courage to change the things I can; and the wisdom to know the difference."

—REINHOLD NIEBUHR, SERENITY PRAYER

One of the phrases I hear clients parrot back to me frequently is, "I know, it's not *my* backpack!" This phrase went viral when I began my work as an organizational life coach at Delta Defense. When I shared the backpack philosophy, employees began using it to guide their personal and professional boundaries. The uncertainty about how to operate from clear boundaries circled our conversations repeatedly. What are the right boundaries? What if others don't accept my boundaries and problems escalate? These questions infiltrate our minds on a regular basis. The backpack phrase quickly became a motto for change. Clients have shared that even their family members say it back to them now. Every time I hear it, I can't help but smile.

The backpack philosophy helps to teach awareness and regulation of emotional boundaries, keys to emotional intelligence. Out of concern for loved ones, from the defensive nature of our desire to be right, and in justification of our principles, we become easily affected by the behavior of others. We live in a world of strong personalities and opinions about how we should live as individuals and groups. Politically we are divided more than ever, fighting to be right and led by agenda and experiential bias. We have conflict between the emotional empaths and heavy no-nonsense logics.

Based on how you were raised, your perception of reality and your moral compass develops. But whose perception is accurate? Each of us carries our own bias, led by *our* experience. Boundaries are often unclear because of the assumptions triggered by emotion. Judgment spreads easily with opposing views. Left-brained individuals are perceived as lacking empathy. Right-brainers are thought of as overly emotional. Those who have experienced trauma are viewed as fragile. People with wealth are considered entitled. But are these perceptions true? The truth is that we don't truly know and understand other people. Not fully. Our insight needs to be focused on our growth patterns over time, not focused on what others think, say, or do. How well you understand and move through your emotional pain is your responsibility, so that you can skillfully communicate with others.

I have read and shared Brené Brown's research. She has changed our world through education on topics of empathy, shame, gratitude, bravery, and leadership. Her literary work highlights our attention to the stories we tell ourselves, justifying why we either intervene in the problems around us or choose not to. How we frame difficulties in our mind drives opinions and beliefs. Based on experience, the stories you create in your mindset direct your attitude and behavior.

For example, if your story is: "this (situation) is not my business," you are likely to pull away and avoid discussion, disengaging from the topic. However, if you experienced family relationships where members shouted opinions about almost everything, you may have a different attitude. The story that you have in your mind directs your path.

We don't often think about our stories until we slow down enough to ask ourselves questions like:

- What is the story I am telling myself about this situation?
- Is it accurate and helpful?
- Does this situation belong to me?
- How much emotional energy do I need to give to this?

These reflection questions create boundaries for your behavior and how you interact with others.

When our internal motivation lies in the need to be right, we get stuck in relationship dilemmas which lead to venting, gossip, and secret frustration. Being validated by others falsely tells us that our perception is right. I believe it is why we justify venting to friends and feeling this as a connection. We like what is comfortable and predictable. It can be enjoyable being in the business of others, even if our intentions are selfless. It's human nature. As we reflect and understand our experiences as a guide to our motivations, we learn a path that leads to accepting and understanding others more accurately.

Our boundaries are important in defining who we are as individuals. They are the foundation for enjoying peaceful relationships. Boundaries support our mindset, helping us let go of that which does not belong to us and guiding us to focus on what we have control over: ourselves.

When boundaries are loose, we take on the problems of others. When boundaries are rigid, we lack understanding about the needs of others. Identifying the moments when you need to tighten or loosen your grip is when your insight develops.

THE BACKPACK PHILOSOPHY

"Your personal boundaries protect the inner core of your identity and your right to choices."

—GERARD MANLEY HOPKINS

Imagine meeting up with a friend in a coffee shop for a visit. When it is time to leave, you would carefully take your items with you, leaving behind the items that belong to your friend. If I had my backpack (or belongings) with me, I would pick it up as I go on my way. I would not leave it behind with you. Nor would you leave your items behind for me to take home. We wouldn't intentionally steal each other's possessions as we left. However, we do this "emotional" taking all the time and justify it. For example, if you disclose what you are struggling with, it does not belong to me. It belongs to you. My thoughts, feelings, perceptions, and needs are not yours to figure out. Now, this doesn't mean you stop caring about the struggles of others. If you are a loving person, of course, you care. Being empathetic and supportive is healthy. We care deeply, but we don't have to give someone else's experience repetitive "airtime" in our heads, carrying it as our hardship.

When we get caught up in the emotions of others, it leads to our own emotionality, often resulting in judgment and double-standard opinions. However, when we see others as competent individuals, we accept that they are capable of figuring out their struggles, just as we are capable in ours. The perspectives of others belong to them. And yours belong to you. Staying out of the extremes of overreacting (circling strong emotion and judgment) and underreacting (apathy and detachment) leads to secure, balanced emotion. It is challenging to give healthy support to others when we lack our own balance with emotion.

We understand a limited portion of others' struggles but believe we understand it all when personal information is shared. Our opinions tell us this, leading us to believe that our "expert" roles as parents, friends, mentors, supervisors, family members, leaders, and teachers entitle us to share opinions. In reality, we have no idea what another person is dealing with in their personal situation, even after they disclose perspective on it. We do not know the complexity of their experience or circumstances. We know only what we see, based on our backpack experience. Having opinions about others is danger-ous and often ignorant for this very reason. We see a snapshot of a big picture. Our perceptions, riddled with bias, come from our experiences (both good and bad), not from fact. Be careful about sharing opinions because you hold only your experience as perspec-tive. This is why gossip is toxic and often inaccurate. When we share information that does not belong to us, driven by the need to be heard, we cross that line.

Perceptions are not reality. Although they are our reality, they are not a full reality. If you are passionate about your beliefs, it is sometimes challenging to understand why others have such oppos-ing views. When we accept that others can have different ways of thinking, we reduce judgment and ask questions to understand. Curiosity about differences is more productive than merely sharing your opinion, expecting others to think like you. This approach is a gift that opens up your experience, humbles the self, and brings connection.

What belongs to you has to do with *you*. Remember your backpack contains your:

- Thoughts
- Feelings
- Beliefs
- Values
- Perceptions
- Standards
- Expectations
- Needs
- Goals
- Hopes

What belongs to others is *exactly* the same. Honoring this boundary feels intrinsically right. When we don't honor it, it is carried in our backpacks in the form of emotional baggage. Worry, stress, irritation, judgment, and frustration are added weights that we need not carry. Operating from the notion of what belongs to you creates a paradigm that encourages healthy boundaries, particularly around difficult moments. This boundary dilemma can be observed in family relationships, as well as in organizations and larger systems. When this backpack concept gets applied, whether on a micro- or macro-level, it produces meaningfulness that changes who we are and how we interact with others.

Think about all the areas where you observe judgment. Consider your opinions on the following:

- How others spend time or money
- Career choices
- Educational standards
- Family relationships
- Religion
- Politics
- Sports

The list goes on. Assess for yourself when you get caught up in the backpacks of others. Do you experience this boundary violation with family and friends? If so, you can change it.

COVID-19 is a great example of boundary difficulties. It is so common for people to be in the backpacks of others in today's world. I spent time observing how people chose to manage their pandemic situation. I saw two extreme groups of people shouting the loudest. I watched those in great fear of getting and spreading the virus. This group of people openly judged those who weren't following extreme quarantine restrictions. They were isolated in their homes, scrubbing every surface, and avoiding all contact from anyone. All items that came into their homes were purchased online and they lived in continual fear, talking about it constantly. These individuals believed every media report, sharing and shouting on social media sites. I called this group the COVID fear promoters. Living in continual fear, this group was irritated by those not living in complete isolation. Attaching to uncertainty and worst-case scenarios led to obsessive behavior and social media propaganda.

On the other side were the cynical, "this-is-a-hoax" suspicious, angry people who refused to comply with safety guidelines with an "I'll show you" mentality. In this group, people refused to be told what to do and they believed nothing that was reported. They verbalized disgust and anger for any restrictions, denying the validity of the virus. They mocked the mask wearers, hand scrubbers, and those who believed in maximum isolation to reduce the spread. I called this group the COVID angry resisters, stuck in conspiracy theories and internal rage for losing their rights.

Are you noticing the all-or-nothing categories here? The moderate middle was somewhere in between. In this category, no shouting was necessary. The moderates trusted that others were smart enough to know what was right for them. People were free to feel or think as they did, based on their community experience, not supporting fear or resistance. They chose to be wise, generally following the social distance rules without being extreme or fearing outcomes. The members of this group, the COVID moderates, were careful without obsession, and focused on what they were doing without complaining. They continued to live their lives with peaceful middle ground thinking and common sense.

Compliant without fear, the COVID moderates were discerning

without worrying what others thought. Knowing what belonged to them, they spent little time focusing on what other people were doing. They intentionally made pandemic decisions in accordance with their level of comfort, accepting the choices of others based on their circumstances as well. Clear with their choices, based on what was happening in their community, the moderates did their part without preaching or prosecuting. It is unfortunate that the majority were not in this category.

In hindsight, I observed a great deal of complaining and judging. I witnessed right fighting (fighting based on emotion) on media sites and anger resulting from disagreements. Based on personal bias, the extreme groups shouted opinions seeking validation from others who shared their mindset. Shouting loudly gets attention, not respect. Shouting results in division. True courage does not involve pointing fingers in blame, but rather in asking questions to understand a perspective other than your own. I believe this is why we have so much separation in our families, communities, and world. Listening and understanding brings connection. If each of us has the "right" way of doing things, then we stay divided. When we challenge our beliefs, patiently understanding differences and accepting when things don't go "our way," we have an opportunity to apply the backpack boundaries. Accepting what is out of our control guides us away from needing to shout, leading us to choose a peaceful path to seek alignment and walk forward.

Division is why the backpack philosophy is so important. What belongs to you is connected to *your choice*. You live your risk, consequence, emotional experience, and mindset. If you used COVID time to get home projects done, learn a new skill, or wear out your comfy clothes, the choice was yours. If you spent it worrying, judging, or complaining, the choice was also yours. Focus on your backpack. If you carry everyone else's crap, your bag will be awfully heavy. If you don't carry your backpack, others around you will and you'll wear them down. Carry your own!

I recall a personal mission statement shared by one of my clients. It is a quote by Juansen Dizon: "Not everything that weighs you down is yours to carry." Deciding what you will carry is a choice, even if someone else tries to stick stuff in your backpack.

Let's look at a benign situation like driving. If you observe someone driving in a way that you don't like, think about how quickly you can find your way to frustration. Within seconds you might emotionally escalate, venting to others afterward, making assumptions about a situation that you know very little about. If someone else is driving poorly, does that belong to you? Do you need to have an opinion on this? Can sharing your opinions be a form of entitlement? The answer is yes.

A healthy person notices rising internal frustration in situations outside of their control. Accepting a moment of struggle while intentionally directing focus on what belongs to you is a learned skill. However, this is no easy task. Recognizing your mindset errors is critical to your emotional intelligence. Noticing your blind spots requires practice. What others think and do (even if it is about you) has little to do with you. It does not need your attention.

When faced with an emotional situation, beginning from this insight creates clarity. Before reacting, take a moment to reflect.

Ask yourself:

- "Which part of this situation belongs to me?"
- "How do I feel about it? Is my reaction warranted?"
- "What do I need in this situation?"

- "How can I communicate my needs skillfully?"

Creating clear solutions in the energy of your best self is centered on understanding perspective, rather than being right. This process promotes peace of mind. Best-self mindset is driven by connection and dual in nature.

It involves:

1. Doing what you know is healthy and right.
2. Speaking your truth clearly and calmly if/when it is warranted.

When we communicate based on what we feel is wanted by others, we lose our ability to operate authentically.

Take for example an argument with a loved one. Let's say you disagree with something that they are doing. This practice creates an instant boundary for you to hold your tongue, unless the other person specifically asks you to examine what's in their backpack for purposes of growth and connection. Your job is not to fix what you think they need to change. When you make another's struggle yours, you add your own stuff for them to carry in their backpack. *You are not entitled to be heard*, even if that is what you want. The need to place your opinion on others is about you, not them. In this instance, your hands are in their backpack. Even though your opinion is disguised in "but I care" clothing, it is unnecessary unless requested. This is a hard lesson to apply in emotionally charged situations. Trust me, I am not perfect at it either. I just know that this boundary is healthy.

If someone brings you into their problem (asks for your help) and you are there willingly, walk next to them as they carry their backpack and while you carry yours. No one has a better or worse backpack. Each person has a different collection of items they carry around. Begin to notice when you attach to what others are feeling or doing. In these moments you are in violation of this boundary. Likewise, when you do things for others that they can do for themselves, again you are in violation. These boundaries are especially difficult when it comes to adult children, family members, and close friends. Walk next to your people. Don't pull them, push them, or pick up their bag. They are capable.

To be clear, I am not talking about kind gestures that provide support or encouragement. I am referring to the frequent "giving" choices you do as a pattern or expectation because they are not living successfully on their own. For example, if you have an adult child, but you are cleaning for them, paying for things financially, or "taking care" of their adult responsibilities because you feel bad for their struggles, you are contributing to their skill deficit. This form of codependency disguises itself in love, but it is self-concerning at the core and reinforces the problem.

Another example would be taking on the responsibility of someone on your team who is not doing their job, leaving you to perform yours and theirs. This "giving" comes across as a selfless act, but by not addressing the issue with a just resolve, you are left to be an overworked martyr with a patterned unhealthy teammate working below potential. Because this dynamic isn't healthy, regardless of the reason for extending yourself beyond your duties, you can communicate skillfully to stop the problematic pattern. This holds true in almost every relationship.

Let's do one more example. Take someone in the family who is chronically dramatic and negative. I think we can all relate to that! Often when it is family, we react by complaining to others, pandering to make the drama stop, or simply coping with that person, leaving the situation irritated. This pattern could be indefinite until boundaries are laid out clearly and lovingly. When boundaries are not set clearly, the pattern continues producing Einstein's definition of insanity (doing the same thing over and over and expecting a different result). By using the backpack analogy, you peacefully focus on your choice, not theirs.

In some circumstances, when boundaries are defined, it upsets those around you. When this occurs, your loved one might resist or make guilt statements to let you know they are upset. I refer to this as getting hit with their backpack. As limits are established, your loved one may be angry or take it personally. This reaction does not belong to you, either. We can become emotionally skilled at accepting the reactions of others, pivoting in a new direction. By stepping out of the way, we create space to reset an unhelpful interaction pattern. It is important to clearly verbalize boundaries on what you will do and what you won't.

The fear that we will make others upset when creating boundaries can be paralyzing. Most will accept boundaries if they are said in a peaceful and loving energy. Of course, there will always be those who resist limits, even when said beautifully. But again, that does not belong to you. It's not your backpack. You can walk away from any problematic interaction with peace of mind, knowing that you followed your boundary, letting go of the reactions of others. You don't have control over anyone else. Just you. See how that works?

THE MANTRA INSIDE MY BACKPACK

"If you do what you've always done, you'll get what you've always gotten."

—TONY ROBBINS

Growing up in a small blue-collar Wisconsin town in the seventies, life was quite different than it is today. There were bars on every corner and kids riding bikes across town without helmets or shoes. We had no internet or smart electronics. Although many families had big console televisions as the center of their living rooms, digital streaming services were missing staples. We didn't have organic food, specialty coffee drinks, or fitness centers. Worries of identity theft and social media cyberbullying were not a part of life. We had Polaroid memories from poor pixel images and forgotten baby books with faded pictures taped in them.

Life was full of preservatives and unknown risks for disease. Most had beds full of water instead of comfortable, cooling memory foam. Parenting included spankings and tough love, freedom to roam your community on your bicycle (as long as you were home by dark), and getting your mouth washed out with soap when you were disrespectful. People didn't use words like grit, emotional intelligence, or neuroplasticity.

The world was simpler, but not necessarily better. We didn't discuss inclusivity or vulnerability. No one could predict the changes coming from technological advancement. Working from home and instant access to information were not a part of daily life. I guess we didn't know how much our lives would change. As I reflect, I can see how many advances have made our existence better. Hindsight leads to innovation. Change is never all good or all bad. Developments bring exciting new experiences and also dangers.

True change comes from learning from mistakes, being growth-minded, and living peacefully in your present moment. Our internal struggles come from regulating all three areas. I believe no one does this exceptionally well. Keeping aware of the interplay of past, present, and future nurtures our well-being. When you learn to understand the emotional experiences that live deeply in your backpack, while simultaneously practicing best-self habits, you develop core alignment. Learning to do this can feel like a lot of work. Being aware and regulated is not easy. Overreacting, shutting down, or avoiding that which makes us uncomfortable is easier. But who says life should be easy?

The world changes at such a rapid pace that it's hard to keep up with the growth curve. I was fortunate to grow up in a dysfunctional and low-income home, as it taught me the values of not needing much, while at the same time providing a push to develop above the standard of those around me. I often related to television characters. I felt close to author Laura Ingalls Wilder from her accounts in *Little House on the Prairie* about her small town of Walnut Grove, striving to find experiences that led me to something just a little bit better. I was Marilyn Munster (from *The Munsters*), who just didn't seem to fit into her sweet, yet interesting, family. Despite my differences, I kept my cheery disposition, which eventually led to meeting people who would eventually change and rock my world.

I am far from exceptional in any facet of my life. I see myself as a dedicated psychotherapist fascinated by the ever-evolving human condition. I compulsively look for ways to grow and develop the life I have been given. I am not the perfect wife, mother, daughter, friend, sister, Christian, or citizen. My head is often in the clouds and I can be a communication disaster from time to time. What I *have* learned, I struggle to use consistently and timely. Despite the struggle, I persist. This internal battle has fueled my dedication to mindfulness and self-exploration. Most days I live in a purpose-driven battle to balance my old habit train tracks with new, retrained and mindful ones that encourage awareness for living in my best self.

I have persevered through a challenging childhood. In a faithful walk with God, I have felt healing through the love of one man and our life of raising three beautiful daughters. Through many professional years in mental health, I have developed paradigms and practices to wellness.

For over a decade my colleagues and clients encouraged me to document the tools I share, pressing me to write this book. When I met my current boss, this dream became a reality. I watched client after client use these tools to make their lives happier and healthier. I believe we can all develop our internal skills to make life better, learning to live at our fullest potential.

Anyone who knows me well is quick to recite the mantra I have lived my life by: *whatever you pay attention to grows.* I don't know where I heard it or when I recited it for the first time, but this mantra means something so deep to me that I could never fully explain its impact on my life. Furthermore, I know that I am not a master at keeping alignment with this wisdom. It has been my mission statement of wellness for my adult life. I have said it almost every day of the past twenty-five years and it will be the statement of purpose that I have shared to exhaustion.

I knew from a young age that suffering leads to discovery. Intentional choices, despite the emotional pain that accompanies suffering, are the heart of wisdom. *Hearing information leads to knowledge. Applying learning through the struggle leads to wisdom.* I understood hardship early. I am grateful for the wounds in my backpack that gave me strength and purpose. I watched people in my family struggle way more than I did as a result of emotional pain. I thank God every day for His abundant, undeserved blessings. I have consistently believed that things happen to teach us life lessons. I know with certainty that God has led me along my path every step of the way.

As a child I knew that my family was different from those of my friends. We were a community foster family from the time I was in middle school. I recall being exposed early to those suffering mental illness and addiction. I observed this in my mother's family and in the foster care system helping the children we served. I witnessed young children go in and out of homes, many with serious trauma, wounded by violence and neglect. My mother grew up in a family normalized by trauma, sharing her childhood of emotional, physical, and verbal abuse. I witnessed unhealthy relationship boundaries, observing those around me make decisions based on their unmanaged emotion. My witness to these trauma narratives created strong internal fear of trusting people, while at the same time, a high motivation to change family systems.

As I grew into adulthood and became fascinated with psychology, I feared reexposure to the negative events of my past, triggering a desire to prevent chaos in my newly created family. I believe that my anxiety of repeating this generational poison unintentionally led me to blocking emotion rather than feeling it and working through it. This pattern led to controlled behaviors rooted in fear of making mistakes as a wife and mother. I observed myself in difficult moments, paralyzed by the possibility that my emotions would bubble up and somehow turn me into one of the emotional offenders from my childhood. I was afraid of becoming narcissistic, hurtful, and mean, like I witnessed others around me to be. However, with awareness and regulation tools, I eventually understood that my fear was holding me back from experiencing life to its fullest.

With God's good grace, I sought understanding of wellness not only for my clients, but also for myself. I was a sponge, learning as many tools as I could get my hands on. After decades of client teaching and professional mentoring, I practiced setting boundaries and self-acceptance. Over time, the principles I shared became my paradigm too. I will be forever grateful for the honor of being with my clients. For little did they know that I was growing with them in parallel, as they worked on their goals and they inspired me in mine.

Soon my backpack was led by my mission statement: whatever you pay attention to grows. I wanted to pay attention to challenging new experiences, loving my family, and being the happy person that I am at my core. I needed meaningful friendships and servant leadership. I sought peace in my thoughts, consistency in my self-care, and relationships that brought positive energy. I needed to pay attention to consistent wellness. This is *my backpack*. I taught and applied healthy boundaries, surrendering control and focusing solely on my choice in order to be happy. When I intentionally decided to carry my backpack only, the internal struggle subsided.

The process of figuring out what belongs to us and what we are going to pay attention to in any given difficulty is such a gift. When we understand and apply this consistently, we are led toward peace and joy. This power belongs to us. When we stop giving energy to insecurity and negative emotion, we find peace in managing our boundaries. It's an exciting walk that teaches us to let go. As a result, it forces us to frame situations helpfully, living mindfully in the moment. I want this for you, too! I want you to take time to understand what is in your backpack and carry it securely.

Our mindset comes from what we choose to focus our emotional energy on in any given circumstance. This can be practiced with any goal. If you want to improve your self-esteem, enhance a relationship, develop your career path, improve parenting, make friends, get physically fit, or learn a new hobby, it applies. Often our problematic thinking and emotions come from automatic habits, not intentional ones. When you learn awareness, it can become the best muscle you develop. This skill is key to learning how to regulate stress. Without regulation you are left with consequences such as risks for disease, conflict, and chronic unhappiness.

We will never enjoy the discomfort of emotional pain; however, living its purpose is helpful to our meaningful growth. We grow because of pain. It makes us, not breaks us. It develops our character, keeping us humble and strong. It has been a gift to me, providing the avenue to emotional security that I need and celebrate today. I am so grateful for all those who nurtured my development. They believed in me and helped me understand my backpack in order to create a framework for others to understand theirs. I want to pay forward my lessons and tools to help others who struggle with believing that change is possible.

My backpack mantra saved me from a life of misery, placing me on the road to joyful meaning. Regardless of circumstance we have choice in how we react, the mindset we choose, and the path we walk. It doesn't matter what is going on around us. What others are doing need not be a factor in our decisions. What matters is what we choose, moving through difficulty skillfully. This insight *is* the backpack philosophy.

Emotional intelligence guides us toward awareness and regulation, which starves negativity. When we slow down and figure out how to do this, we have direction that changes who we are when difficulties arise. This positive change scatters to others. We can light up this world or add to the darkness in our difficult moments. Living from a mindset of peace and gratitude is more productive. Applying this rule in a moment of emotionality is true wisdom.

We live in a world of energy. What we choose to give energy to leads our path. We have endless opportunities circling us. If we are not careful, we will live in a zone of endless busyness, instead of intentional meaningfulness. Bombarded by information, our minds race from one thing to another. If we do this long enough, it becomes normal and the stories in our mind justify the pattern of being busy constantly. Before long, we are overwhelmed and tired, losing emotional presence. This pattern of running from one thing to another, followed by shutting down in complete exhaustion, is a common problem. This energy battle breeds anxiety and depression as habits, which then need to be retrained. If you are like me, you find yourself questioning what should (and shouldn't) get emotional attention in your mind. Can you relate?

After years of coaching wellness, I found myself creating a toolbox of skills and resources that anyone can use. I observed those struggling with anxiety and depression in frequent preoccupation with the behavior of others who triggered their negative reactions. It is my hope and desire for you to stop battling internally about what others are doing around you. I want you to make your mind a place of peace, understanding clearly what belongs to you, and navigating your emotions with certainty.

I am a simple girl who came from little means, believing in those who take responsibility for their choices to live a healthy life. My purpose is to share what I know. Some may agree. Others won't. But that doesn't matter to me. I know these tools work. I have seen it in clinical practice year after year. When I shared my emotional boundaries theory of the backpack with my clients, many encouraged me to write this book because the tools changed their lives. If you want to be clear about your boundaries, then walk with me through this book, carrying your backpack. Life gets easier when you know and focus on what belongs to you.

THE WELLNESS GPA FORMULA

"The concept of total wellness recognizes that our every thought, word, and behavior affect our greater health and well-being. And we, in turn, are affected not only emotionally but also physically and spiritually."

—GREG ANDERSON

Anxiety is a habit reaction that occurs as a result of repetitive thoughts or feelings stored in the brain from a sensory or external trigger. Most people can relate to having anxiety of some kind, but many do not know how to retrain that system's response.

One of the tools that I have used in clinical practice has been the Wellness GPA. As a young clinician, I spent time diagnosing problems more than treating wellness. When I began using this formula, rooted in cognitive behavioral therapy (CBT), it became a tool for assessing emotional well-being and a formula for regulating it simultaneously.

When I was in high school, my GPA was important to me. It represented the outcomes of my academic standing. It was a metric that gave me control over something positive in my life. After years of coaching wellness, I found myself using this grading scale for clients. The Wellness GPA works like this: it assesses a person's well-being, while also providing a map to create solutions for growth. Three areas that show wellness and dysfunction are as follows:

1. Emotional response to stress, observed in the reaction system of the body.
2. Mindset response to stress found in thoughts, internal dialogue, personal beliefs, and the stories that frame experiences.
3. Choices, specifically behavioral patterns, self-care, and communication with others around stressful events.

I found this three-prong tool useful in building accurate self-awareness. Self-appraisal is often inaccurate. Our errored perceptions develop from fear of saying the truth, the distortions we learn and repeat, and defenses rooted in fear and insecurity. It's much easier to notice what others are doing wrong, rather than assess how well you are managing your backpack in the emotionally triggered situation. We tend to do what we always do.

Generally, people know what triggers their varying moods. They can often identify the problems that circle around them. When we notice what is going wrong, we quickly find blame and focus on what others should do differently to make our experience better. This negative pattern sets up a human need for blocking emotion, numbing out, and avoiding what makes us uncomfortable. It can lead to ruminating on "what if" probabilities and "why is this happening" thoughts, reinforcing a state of misery. This pattern creates the thinking loop of noticing when others are irritating us, and next, reacting in judgment. However, when a person focuses exclusively on their part, keeping intentional alignment with their values, misery passes. Without this awareness, strong emotions lead the triggered experience, eventually creating a pattern of overreacting or avoiding, blocking growth.

Furthermore, the cycle continues from trigger, to reaction, to negative thought (either in justification or blame), to impulse. This pattern can seep into your personality as your normal experience. The repeated pattern of this cycle affects our relationships with others. It interrupts personal and professional experience. Misery is often the result of how we see ourselves, others, and our circumstances.

I have learned that it is not the symptoms one experiences that dictate wellness. It is how one navigates and assigns meaning to experience that matters. I have met so many people affected by challenging symptoms and overwhelming circumstances. Their ability to skillfully navigate through these situations inspires me to share the gifts that come from hardship.

I had a female client named Maggie years ago who suffered from post-traumatic stress disorder (PTSD) as a result of childhood sexual abuse that likely contributed to domestic violence in her dating relationships. She entered therapy with me in her early twenties after a significant death in her family. For two years, she attended weekly counseling to work through loss, understand her trauma, and change her self-image. She was abusing alcohol heavily at the time, living in shame and self-hatred. Unresolved trauma surfaced in strong appearance insecurities, codependent patterns of enabling her boyfriends, and chronic stomach and migraine pain. She initially resisted setting boundaries in fear of how others would react.

Maggie worked to understand how her unresolved trauma impacted how she thought and cared for self, specifically how she avoided boundaries out of fear. Over time she tackled her insecurities, learning healthy ways to work through anxiety triggers. When she chose to revisit her memories with the intention of healing, she could own the strength and resilience that came from her trauma, restructuring thoughts of personalized shame. After aligning her reactions, thoughts, and choices, she was able to see herself differently, executing new boundaries in her relationships. She monitored her Wellness GPA, growing skills and creating alignment with her values. Maggie didn't know who she was until she unpacked her backpack. We can overcome anything with the right mindset and tools.

I have journeyed with clients from those experiencing temporary symptoms and normal life hurts to those with severe mental illness and extraordinary tragedy. Some pursue growth while others settle for unhappiness or something in between. How people think is a key factor in whether they live in peace. I think it is why some can be negative in normal life irritations such as driving, waiting in a long line, or how a person loads a dishwasher. When faced with a triggered stress, the way we dialogue internally outlines the path for either misery or acceptance, peace or frustration.

For example, if I am late due to a traffic issue, I can sit in anger and criticism of the drivers who surround me or use that time meaningfully in a way that gives peace. If I choose to listen to an audiobook to learn a new skill or enjoy music, I shift perspective. When you focus on what could go wrong, you hop on the thinking train to frustration rather than seeing it as an opportunity to gain something that you need. You can teach yourself to experience negative situations helpfully. I challenge you to try this with something that frustrates you. Applying this opens up a pathway of opportunity. I find joy in watching the light bulb moments with clients learning regulation tools, observing the peacefulness that follows retrained connections.

You can choose to let go of your judgments about others. They come from habit and lack awareness. When frustrated by differences of opinion, you can learn to pivot away from the many things that are not your business. The choices of others are not your business. You practice negativity without noticing because it is normal and acceptable in your social circles. When you observe these moments, your perspective changes.

We live in a world of high judgment. There are socially acceptable rules for everything. This list includes relationships, professionalism, lifestyle, fashion, and so on. We love it when people like, think, and believe as we do. Face it, it's validating "being right" and it provides a false sense of belonging. Because this reinforcement feels good, it keeps us in our comfort zone. It's how our ego grows over time. The more we are right, the more we want to be right. When skilled at anything, it comes at a price of wanting to preach that expertise, which perpetuates our ego. It is an unconscious paradox—developing skill and creating automatic judgment with mastery.

Let's examine mastery with judgment (ego connected) versus discernment (choice connected). Discernment is about "the whys" of your choice. Judgment involves attachment to the emotional reaction connected to another's choice. When we focus solely on our choice, we let go of the unneeded emotion. This process replaces judgment with a neutral, healthy choice.

Let's apply this three-tier GPA awareness tool for managing stress. It can be a formula used to reset the brain habit that activates the fight or flight response during a stressful moment. One of the primary tools I teach is to practice the Body-Mind-Choice formula (using the Wellness GPA pillars) for managing stressful situations. This tool can regulate emotion when it is out of balance in our body. I encourage people to acknowledge all three parts for alignment among the body's emotional center, the brain's thought center, and the new habit behavior one is seeking.

BODY-MIND-CHOICE FORMULA

Body (slowing down or speeding up energy to reset the body's internal imbalance)

Mind (awareness of negative thoughts, refocusing on productive ones)

Choice (productive behavior aligned with intention, not the triggered emotion)

When we are triggered to a stress reaction, we feel it in our body. Stress typically shows itself through symptoms of body discomfort. Symptoms may include: a flush of adrenaline, racing thoughts and heart, difficulty concentrating, digestive issues, body pain, and sweating. This internal flooding leads to our brain spinning with racing thoughts creating a shutdown in our emotional presence. The process produces anxiety, encouraging us to leave the situation we are facing.

Let's put this into practice. The first step in a stress moment is to recognize your adrenaline surge and *slow your body down*. When a trigger occurs, your body's system amps up, creating an alarm that sends it into false panic. When this occurs, thoughts become irrational, leading to escalation or avoidance. Slowing down breathing and relaxing muscles helps to change this fight or flight reaction, allowing it to reduce speed, relax, and reset into balance.

Stress reactions cause us to lose our emotional presence, creating a habit or pattern of feeling overwhelmed and scattered. We can develop grounding habits through slow breathing in these moments. By checking in with your sensory surroundings and intentionally relaxing, you have the ability to reroute the process that sends you toward negative thinking. It's about finding the optimal balance zone, where the body again is peaceful. For those who block this adrenaline flow, they often feel detached and numb, which pulls them out of observing and managing emotions in a helpful way.

When I learned this skill, I used the breathing cube as my guide: a six-second slowly inhaled breath, holding for six counts, and a six-count slow exhale of breath, done six times. As you slow your breathing rhythm, you relax each part of your body from head to toe. The efficacy of this tool takes repeated practice, but it is worth it if you patiently stick to it. I learned this in a college dance class decades ago. I still use it today.

Once the body slows down, shifting your mind to a helpful thought can direct it from discomfort to peace. This second tier of *fixing mindset* helps to create movement toward a better way of thinking. Most often, negative beliefs are paired with negative body reactions, fueling the fight or flight response that leads to unproductive urges. In the midst of reaction, our brains seek release through venting, shutting down, or irritability behaviors. A helpful mantra repeated in your self-talk redirects the negative thoughts away from the body's reaction to an intentional choice, creating internal alignment.

For example, if I am overwhelmed by the number of tasks I have to do, I can take a slow-down break, recognizing that I am overwhelmed and needing to redirect myself. I can direct this process by saying, "I'm going into my focus zone, getting as much done as I can in the next two hours." Rather than ruminating on "there is no way I am going to get all this done," my productive paradigm provides encouragement and meaning to daunting emotions. If you listen to your "inner critic" voice, you are likely to end up on the couch for hours in a mind-numbing activity.

Using a ten-scale score approach can be useful when resetting the mind. Ask yourself how much emotional energy you choose to give to any difficult issue. On a scale of one to ten, with ten representing serious impact situations (death of a loved one, serious injury, health scare with your child, etc.), what score accurately accounts for the energy this situation deserves? The ten-scale tool is a quick and easy way to shift your focus on what gets power over your mood.

Your internal dialogue either creates a pattern toward wellness or disorder. When you notice your negative self-talk, you will have the ability to walk out of the stress moment, returning to peacefulness. Making a list of helpful mindset phrases can shift your thinking in a productive direction when triggered to emotion. If you review those messages daily for the next month, they will direct where your mind goes in frustrating moments.

Finally, the third part of this formula is about *creating the intentional choice*, which brings you back into balance. When the body and mind are regulated, it is easier to lean into a choice connected to your big-picture intention. If you don't, your habit center takes over, calling up a negative response familiar in past stress events.

When overwhelmed, we feed off of our adrenaline. One negative thought can lead to another and soon the snowball effect has occurred, feeding thoughts in an irrational loop. If I am late for work, my anxious thoughts can circle ideas of losing my job, others viewing me as incompetent, and even leading to financial disaster scenarios. Negative thoughts spiral quickly.

When body and mind are moving skillfully toward intention, you can direct your mind to alignment with personal values. When in alignment, your decision becomes about *who* you are, rather than what anyone else thinks or wants you to do. If your choice for resolve is not in alignment with your values, it is the wrong choice. As you take the time to slow down and think it through, you productively solve your dilemma.

Let's apply this. Let's say you are intensely overwhelmed. With racing thoughts circling your many responsibilities, you have a panic attack while driving. Your brain will remember this intense fear, automatically calling it up the next time you are ready to get into your car. The fear of having another panic attack could result in the avoidance of driving. Even though this is understandable, is it realistic and helpful? Getting back into the vehicle again quickly requires your willingness to sit in that triggered fear, creating alignment in all three of these areas. If you honor fear, it will paralyze you. Instead, get back in your car quickly. Slow down your breathing, accepting this challenge. Create a mindset that is capable of overriding panic with practice, giving power to your choice to conquer the fear, rather than the fear itself. You will have to do this over and over, but you will rise above it with perseverance. Body-Mind-Choice—it is your tool for conquering anything that has a hold on you.

THE STORIES THAT JUSTIFY

"When we deny our stories and disengage from tough emotions, they don't go away; instead, they own us, they define us. Our job is not to deny the story, but to defy the ending—to rise strong, recognize our story, and rumble with the truth until we get to a place where we think, Yes. This is what happened."

—BRENÉ BROWN

We are creatures of habit, believing our perceptions, rooted in past experiences. But what happens when we decide to challenge our paradigms and do something different for the purpose of expanding our well-being? Regardless of the level of difficulty, we can retrain how we manage any situation. Although this concept is simple, we are enslaved to our status quo "normal" until we decide to change.

Human beings follow habits more than intentions. We learn early in life to create stories in our mind to justify our experiences. As a parent, when our child is naughty, we seek the story that makes us feel better. "My child was just hungry. He didn't get a good nap today." We create stories to justify negative moods and alleviate the discomfort of accurately seeing our flaws or the struggles of those we support. "This wouldn't have happened if _____ wouldn't have done _____ first." We are late because of traffic. Because we didn't sleep well, we become forgetful. Disengagement at work is due to recent family burdens. We make excuses for irritability leading to hurtful words said in frustration. We exaggerate our values and blame honesty: "I was just telling the truth!" Regardless of the circumstance, the mindset we accept dictates our experience.

When we lack follow-through on our intention, it's easy to make excuses because of the circumstances. Take for example my desire to exercise regularly. I genuinely want to work out daily. The thought is present multiple times throughout my day with good intention. Why am I not consistent then? I have the right attitude and multiple opportunities for incorporating this into my routine. I believe exercise is a priority, yet it's the first thing to exclude on my schedule. Others do it. They suggest to "build it into your day" and I parrot this same phrase to my clients who don't follow through. Despite my positive mindset, the story I say in a moment of resistance during the day leads to my outcome.

After a few weeks of consistency, something throws me off. It could be a new priority, a random headache, a preoccupation with an upcoming event, or a dozen other things. It doesn't take much before my mind falsely tells me that as a result of circumstances, I won't be able to follow through with my intention. This fall from consistency happens quickly. Sometimes I don't even know it until after a couple of days have gone by. Does this same pattern happen to you? I bet it does. Maybe not with exercise, but likely with something that is important to you. It's all in the struggle of being a flawed human being.

If you take the time to notice your thoughts, journaling intention, you have greater success. When you focus on barriers, you get obstacles. The sooner you see your capability of getting back on track, the quicker the realignment. I believe this is key. It's not about exercising every day. Or eating perfectly. Success isn't about moving up the corporate ladder by a certain age. Happiness is not automatic because you find the right person or have the perfect job or children. Wellness comes from observing what you do when things are *not* happening according to plan. It is about the emotional tools you use to navigate difficult moments. It's about getting back on track as quickly as possible so that you are managing the situation, resetting toward your baseline best self. It is about regulation, not perfection or failure.

When I came to realize this, I stopped trying to be good enough based on a desired outcome. I am good enough regardless of whether I am achieving my goals in a particular moment. I am good enough whether I am on track or not. So are you, dear friend! Focusing your efforts on getting back on track quickly is the healthier goal. When we are outcome-driven our thoughts focus on problems. Outcome-only plans do not work. If you want to lose weight, create a goal to catch moments when you are off track, pivoting back as quickly as you can. This is better than focusing on how much weight you need to lose. If you have a temper, don't set a goal that you should never lose your cool. The goal should be to notice when you are losing your cool and apologize quickly so you can return to a good attitude and mend the communication timely with the affected loved one.

Examine the goals where you feel off track. What are the excuses that you tell yourself that justify your inconsistent pattern? That justification, which you pay attention to over and over, quickly becomes your reality.

Examine your mindset stories around these areas:

- Why you haven't taken care of yourself consistently
- Why you haven't fixed unhealthy patterns in difficult relationships
- Why you don't discuss important issues at home or work

- Why you procrastinate on important responsibilities

Oh, the many stories that accompany our repetitive patterns! These narratives lead us away from intention, feeding old thoughts, which get the best of us. And let's face it, we believe our excuses time and time again. Until we acknowledge it as an excuse. When we stop, the adventure toward skill development begins. This self-change process is thrilling, meaningful, energy creating, and frustrating all rolled into one. It is not easy, but it's worth it. If you are at this point in your life, set doubt aside and lean into changing what is in your control. You won't regret it. Whatever you focus your energy on will produce the outcome of that intention. Complaining about what is wrong in our life stops when we commit to changing how we see and respond to problems.

Venting frustration comes from a place of self-concern that circles around how a person, situation, or event impacts you. Once you start noticing your unhelpful narratives, you can change your self-talk to acceptance and solutions.

I recall a client who would complain about having a toxic relationship with her sister. Clarissa was a happily married young mother. She had a competitive relationship with a younger sister, who was demanding and hostile when she didn't get her way. This sibling dynamic had been consistent since their youth. In order to keep her sister from "blowing up," Clarissa and her father gave in constantly to the many demands. We discussed her fear of managing her sister's explosive behavior, which nurtured unhealthy boundaries. Clarissa found pleasure in seeking comfort from her father who shared in her secret frustration. For years they would collude on shared irritations, giving in just to keep the peace.

Using the backpack paradigm, we clarified what choices belonged to Clarissa, to her sister, and to her father. The "peace at all costs" family paradigm was an unproductive mental habit that perpetuated her sister's behavior. Clarissa would say, "But she is my sister, what can I do?" She practiced verbalizing clear boundaries rather than focusing on her sister's behavior. Over time, she let go of the fear connected to her sister's reactions and her confidence grew. Clarissa stopped feeding this dynamic with consistent limits. She learned helpful phrases to stop negative conversations and practiced saying "no, thank you" in a calm and peaceful way. Eventually the sister's explosive demands diminished. Although Clarissa's sister wouldn't take responsibility for her part of the change process, a healthier mindset and pattern developed.

We cannot control what others do. However, we can make decisions about what we do and why we do it. When our choices are led by healthy well-being, peace results.

Let's take a step toward examining your past misery moments. If your focus is on the negative behavior of others, you will get stuck in your emotion. Learning to focus on your choice exclusively creates productive decisions. By letting others do as they choose, we manage the situation better because we are carrying only what belongs to us. This process of directing our choice works because it guides us toward who we are, rather than what we want or what we perceive is going on. When we are who-focused (who you are in response to the situation), we seek alignment with our values, freeing us from fears connected to the problem. This directs us toward solutions. Paying attention to your decision and being grounded in your intention clarifies your peaceful inner voice.

Our wellness muscles do not develop organically. They are carefully nurtured over time. It takes practiced observation of the self and consistency with intentional habits to create these patterns that bring us meaningfulness and growth. I believe that no matter what you have been through in your life, you can learn to develop patterns that will lead to peace. The path out of the overthinking misery maze is a rewarding journey. Our emotions and mistakes are teachers, making us work hard in our relationships, providing gifts of personal resilience. When we step out of a dark hole, we are relieved and invigorated. The deeper the hole, the more joy we have in coming out of it. Despite the challenges that this process gives, it opens up new ways of being that only those who struggle to find them, *know*.

The process of shifting from misery to peace develops an internal dialogue that reinforces the inner self. When you decide to focus on your next forward choice, rather than your "in the moment" frustration, you learn to shift from emotion to intention. Your secure voice will help you focus on the present moment, avoiding "the whys," "the what ifs," or "the shoulds" and faulty assumptions of potential bad outcomes, letting worry and fear pass by.

The process of staying emotionally present is like driving over a bridge with guardrails on the overpass. The rails prevent drivers from falling off the edge. Staying close to who you are in your best self creates internal guard rails that prevent fear from taking over. By keeping to your present moment, you can learn to direct the triggered fear response toward a peaceful choice. This approach helps you execute intention that directs you out of the mindset maze, which focuses on others.

The practice of mindful presence is so very apparent to me as our lives have been altered by the COVID-19 quarantine. Working from home has become the new normal. The overplayed media fear and political tactics, and the conversation compulsion on social media sites and telecommunication has brought on many "what if" fears that I observed in others. Fear gained attention in my personal and professional relationships and was a constant reminder in my home, with all the COVID supplies representing a new standard of living. People are justifying and living in fear now more than ever.

While experiencing life in a pandemic, I used my mission statement daily. Getting lost in the fear could have been easy. Maintaining middle ground balance required effort. As I continued to observe, I would check my intention. What do I have control over? I don't have control over what anyone else thinks or feels. I don't have control over what gets reported in the media. I don't have control over anyone other than me. I choose to do my part, pursuing peace. This is what I pay attention to—my backpack. I refused the immersion of constant media. Although this concept of "walking the middle ground" seems simple, I was struck by how others, in the moment of fear, resorted to extremes. It was evidence of the relationship between anxiety and control, which often leads to double standards. My hope is that the pandemic created more quiet time in our world, giving people perspective on what is most important.

We have a spoiled culture with so many amazing freedoms. Despite these blessings, we lack understanding, especially with the emotional boundaries of those around us. We need more compassion, connection, and wisdom. It takes these virtues to be able to apply our beliefs in the moments we need them the most. If we use this pandemic time to appreciate solitude, nurturing our best self, the shift toward perspective begins.

In hindsight, many of us will have gained new skills. We will not take for granted the freedom to go where we want to and see the people we love. However, I know that some will look back on this historic time with a negative lens, seeing it from a self-concerned place, fueling the very problems that keep misery going. Choose to see the good in it, regardless of how it was handled or what others said about it. Let's focus on what this quiet taught us for the greater good and thrive in spite of it. Will our world continue to change? Of course it will. Choose to focus on the lesson, not the inconvenience or divisions.

In my coaching to develop others, I have been honored to nurture so many meaningful relationships with those who have struggled through hardship. At the end of treatment, I ask clients to verbalize what they have learned, identifying specific changes they made. Self-development work is never a waste of time. Closure is typically met with tears of joy, overwhelming peace from needed change, and a sense of relief that the individual is no longer trapped in hurt.

No matter who you are or how you were raised, you can do this work. This meaningful, life-changing work raises the bar in your relationships and impacts the soul. Hearing the wisdom that comes from suffering makes me so grateful for finding this career path. The journey of self-discovery is key to creating intentional habits. Therapy with clients is about rewriting stories that began in hurt and ended in growth. Learning to notice the negativity in your backpack will make a difference in how you interpret your experience and walk with others.

I have watched two types of people. I have seen those who pay attention to suffering, creating patterns of behavior that scatter negativity to others. Conversely, I have observed others who pay attention to regulating misery, which brings joy. Your mindset spills to others. Peace and patience are simply never regretted in the legacy of life. If you visit self-concern often, your attitudes and behaviors reflect it. When you practice regulation, you can get comfortable there, producing outcomes similarly. Frustration is not your destination. It is your point of awareness that gets you to a better destination. Pain is a guide to wellness. It is a gift. It really is!

It is easier to evaluate others than yourself because it is safer emotionally. When you are irritated and jump quickly into judgment, it is often disguised in the clothing of concern. Reflect on moments of irritation or frustration with those around you. Observing emotion helps irritations pass, which is better than creating a story of what someone else needs to do differently. Emotion has power to bring us closer or create distance.

As humans, we tend to believe that we are altruistic in our intentions. When we acknowledge our struggles, we move from justification to insight about why we do what we do. When we are irritated, it is our problem to solve internally, even if the irritant is someone's poor manners. The power we have to influence change does not come from knowledge. Instead, it comes from your mindful attention to your own behavior, regardless of circumstance. When you operate from empathy, you can see that the irritating behavior of others is just like your irritating behavior in different situations than the one you are experiencing in that moment. Focus on your internal change, not judging or preaching. Leading is carrying your backpack skillfully before trying to teach someone else how to carry theirs. When you decide to live in alignment with your values, you will celebrate the differences in others without frustration.

When it comes to relationships, you will never look back on your life and wish that you were not the absolute best person you could be. At the end of your life, you will likely not care about bank accounts, possessions, or status. Name-brand items, fancy homes, and credentials will not define your existence. Instead, you are likely to care about the impact of your relationships as it relates to your purpose.

Take a moment and visualize your most optimal self. Write down the words that come to mind. What qualities do you want others to say about how you lived your life? What are the words that describe your best self? Our legacy is about how consistently and authentically we stay true to those intentions throughout our lifespan, even in moments of intense emotion. Awareness about *who* you are can be nurtured and practiced. Unpacking your best self takes you on a hike of changing self-talk, negative attitudes, and problematic communication.

Notice the moments when you are out of alignment with those values:

- Moments of anger, saying something harsh
- Moments when you avoid uncomfortable situations
- Inappropriate thoughts, unfiltered talk, sexual comments disguised in humor
- Name-calling and high judgment thinking directed at others or yourself
- Dishonesty moments: saying something that isn't true simply because it sounds better or may be received better
- Leading or falling into a gossip train because someone irritates you
- Jealousy moments that lead to insecurity, conflict, or control
- Envy and comparison moments, which lead to judgment and emotional distance
- Self-pity, victim thinking, and martyrdom behavior because of your perceived misfortune
- Guilt thinking loops that nurture shame and sadness
- Greed and unrest, pulling you away from contentment
- Pride moments, preventing you from saying "I am sorry" or "this was my fault" or "please help me; I am stuck"
- Inconsideration and poor awareness of the contributions of others
- Damaging your body and mind by numbing out on unhealthy escape behaviors

There are many examples of misalignment that we rationalize. What can you change to make your life healthier? Whatever that is, do it. Don't wait.

The good, the bad, and the ugly moments in our experiences are meant to teach us. Will you let your past teach you? Your most vulnerable self gives you information about why you do what you do. You can learn to understand the emotional traps that reduce your wellness. Trust me, you will not regret changing yourself. You can develop any emotional skill you lack in this present moment. You can learn to communicate with clear and healthy boundaries, accepting the many things out of your control. With practice you can live in consistent alignment with your values.

Take a moment to think about your backpack. What blame stories do you carry in your backpack? Do those narratives help or hurt you? Put your backpack on and fasten it securely. Walk alongside me as I share my backpack with you.

FOR YOUR BACKPACK

Life is a journey filled with hills and valleys. Your backpack is how you choose to see and walk through your life. Your perspective is based on your experience. Your reactions, thoughts, and choices belong to you.

MY BACKPACK

———

"Anxiety does not empty tomorrow of its sorrows, but only empties today of its strength."

—CHARLES SPURGEON

THE GIFT OF WOUNDS

"Not only so, but we also glory in our sufferings because we know that suffering produces perseverance; perseverance, character, and character, hope."

—ROMAN 5:3–4

I grew up in a small town to a sheltered existence. As an adult I find that my memory is poor about my childhood. I believe it is God's way of providing peace about my past. I often rely on others around me for the things I cannot remember. My older sister has been my memory for a long time. She has amazing recall of the good and bad things from our childhood and I frequently defer to her because I know she will remember names and dates better than I will. I was often in my own little world, which kept me safe and happy. I tend to move fast and juggle a great deal at once, which in some ways has been a saving grace in my life. The downside of this strength is a lack of presence, where details get lost. I have learned to cope with this long term, while at the same time practicing skills to listen. I am sure I am not alone in the battle to be more mindful.

I remember having big moments of happiness and sadness in my childhood, both of which often went unnoticed. Like so many, I was bullied by peers who took pleasure in witnessing my fear. As a kid, I spent time alone, under the steps in my self-made fort listening to music from my boom box and taping songs from Casey Kasem's *American Top 40* radio show. Getting lost in the fantasy of falling in love and having a family of my own occupied my dreams. I spent endless hours locked in our small downstairs bathroom so I could read in quiet.

I recall riding my bike to the neighborhood pond where I would sit by the lilac trees, look up at the billowy clouds, and imagine how life would be when I was all grown up. I can still smell those lilacs in my mind when I take myself back there. I have always been a dreamer, filled with ideas of hope and imagination. To this day, I still enjoy being alone in my thoughts, escaping into music, books, or daydreaming about days to come.

Since early in my life, I have felt that I was strong, even in dark moments. I don't care what others think about me and am not a people pleaser. If you don't like me or agree with me, I accept that. We all walk this life differently. Overall, these are good traits. However, unregulated moments of not caring what others think can lead to inconsideration and poor social awareness, which I have had to work at diligently. Personal contentment lends itself to being inconsistent at initiating connection. Just ask my friends and family. They reach out and coordinate more connections than I do. I love to surround myself with those who do this naturally. Maybe in my geriatric years I will master thoughtfulness with practice. We are never too old to change.

I have always gone after what I want, even if someone else thought it was unattainable. Particularly in this decade of my life, I have spent more time focusing on what I need to do rather than how others feel about it. I trust God's plan and vow to never stop growing and changing the things about me that need adjustment. Accepting my many flaws, I find humor in them and they don't embarrass me like they did when I was younger. I know that I am doing the best I can. I feel God grows me through my flaws. I am blessed richly for the gift of faith at an early age and witnessing God's hand in my story. I am grateful for each person who graces my life, good or bad, because they are my teachers. I choose to be joyful every day. *Let's face it, Holly, you probably annoy the crap out of most people with all that joy and cheer.* Anyone who knows me will chuckle as they read this. I believe that this bubbling joy comes from the messy, interesting life I was given. I am sure that some people are fascinated by this, while others think it is fake. I don't care either way. I am me. Perfectly imperfect. I choose to make the most of this life.

There were important moments in my backpack that helped me understand who I am. I share them for the purpose of making the connections between hardship and strength. You have your own resilient moments in your backpack. Strength comes from how we view our story. I am proud of mine.

When I was little, I remember fearing my maternal grandfather (the man who raised my mother, although not her birth father). He was an angry alcoholic with a foul mouth. He would babysit when my parents went out. I remember begging for teenaged babysitters because they were kind, unlike my grandfather. One evening while he was in charge, I recall witnessing his struggle with rage. Amy and I were tucked into our twin beds, giggling as children do before falling asleep. I don't remember what made us laugh. Grandpa came stumbling into our room cursing, "Why are you goddamned kids making so much noise? You should be sleeping!" Without thinking there would be consequences, my sister responded, "Holly is making me laugh!" A statement likely to be true. Amy had it emotionally rougher than me most days. I enjoyed the role of making her laugh by being silly and utterly outrageous, a quality I still possess today.

Without hesitation, my grandfather grabbed me by the arm, removed his belt, pulled up my nightgown, ripped off my underwear, and beat me until he felt better, throwing me back into bed in his comfortable rage. I cried myself to sleep that night. My sister cried too. I was five years old and she was seven. I don't remember talking about that night again until many years later when we were adults. I know she had her share of traumatic experiences too. We understood each other's pain and got through our tragedies together. In a weird way, I was grateful that she was with me in the room that night. I didn't have to carry that memory alone. I think that is why those affected by trauma, whether momentary or extensive, often understand each other instantly. I am thankful for my sister for being there with me. I am thankful for her love. We will always be close.

This defining moment with my grandfather (along with many others) created an unconscious fear of talking about real feelings with people in my life. Since childhood, I felt I needed to emotionally handle things on my own. Sometimes when you feel strong, the downside is that you push others away in the name of "I can handle this!" Even though it helped me work hard (sometimes too hard), it led me to not ask for what I needed emotionally and put my feelings on the back burner. Asking for help is difficult for me. When I understood the connection between this event and my emotional skill deficit, my backpack got lighter. With intention, I practice asking for help when I need it.

That traumatic experience became one of my best moments. I handled that pain and all the other rough moments that occurred in my family; I am a survivor. There were other hurtful moments that I had to work through, but that one stands out as *the one* that significantly impacted me. I don't hate my childhood. I don't carry blame or resentment. It made me who I am. I choose to see it that way.

My maternal grandmother was just as hateful as her husband. In my youth, I recall my mother disclosing her own childhood experiences of family violence. Grandma had strong jealousy, a deceptive heart, and an arrogant spirit. She and Grandpa would argue abusively and gossip religiously. Every chance she got, she would say terrible things about my loving paternal grandparents, people who were so dear to me. It was exhausting being around her because it required continually being on guard against criticism and covert hostility. Anyone exhibiting these characteristics activates a strong trigger response in me. I quickly move away from those people.

When I was seven, I recall having a sleepover at my maternal grandmother's house where she insisted on feeding me macaroni and cheese at her kitchen table. She force-fed me food that she knew I hated. I remember crying and pleading with her that I couldn't swallow it, while she persisted. Crying hysterically, I gagged down heaping spoonfuls until I vomited all over her kitchen table. This ignited her fury even more. She enjoyed cruelty and I felt it. I hated being around her because I felt her darkness with every contact. She picked at me every chance she could until I stopped interacting with her altogether in my adult years. To others Grandma appeared as an innocent lady, yet I felt her troubled spirit. To this day, I *hate* macaroni and cheese and wooden spoons. I cannot tolerate them in my kitchen, and they make me physically sick.

I did not feel sad when my mother's parents died. My grandfather ended his own life with a shotgun to his head when he was eighty years old. My grandmother lived into her nineties. I have no regret for keeping my distance from them in my adult years. I would not take the risk of their negative behavior affecting my children. This was a boundary that I needed to set, even if others in my life did not understand. The hate they demonstrated encouraged my love. I used their negative example to fuel my positive one. Little did they know that their example of dysfunction motivated my love.

When we were raising our daughters years later, I made a conscious effort to make macaroni and cheese. In some way, it made me feel vindicated that I could prepare a meal that was abusively fed to me, serving it in a loving way to my girls, who would never know this type of emotional pain. My grandmother couldn't rob me of that. Her hate came from *her* backpack, not mine. Just like the belt incident, I learned not to give away my power.

Unhealthy family boundaries led to estrangements and patterns of emotional triangulation in the family. These wounds are gifts when you see them from a mindset of wisdom. Because of the chaos, I became tough. Far from perfect, but not broken. Dear friend, do not let suffering define you. It belongs to the person directing it. Hurt comes from the unsolved pain of others and it should not define your identity. Whatever you pay attention to grows. Will you give attention to your hurts or focus on the life lessons through them?

As I began understanding my backpack, it brought healing. I would not add more pain and misery to the world no matter who started it. Despite the pain, I could not feed hate or regret. Rising above it brought me emotional freedom. It made my backpack lighter.

As a foster sister, I struggled with the internal battle of resentment toward the traumatized children who absorbed the attention of my parents and the desire to help these wounded souls feel seen and heard. This paradox circled my thoughts as a youth. As an acquiescent child, I did not rock the boat at home. But I deeply wanted to be noticed and understood. I learned quickly to mind my own business, figuring things out independently. This lack of direction gave me gifts.

As a teenager, I developed a close bond with one foster brother who lived with us for two years. He was a delightful little boy. He would sneak into the kitchen and drink pickle juice from the jar. I could smell it on his shirt all the time. I loved that he shadowed me about the house riddling me with questions. Physically abused by his stepfather and unprotected by his birth mother, he was caught between the domestic violence at home and the multiple foster placements trying to keep him safe.

I recall my mother urging his caseworker to let him remain in our home when the foster care system decided to reunite him with his birth family. I can still hear her pleading, "But they (his parents) are not ready yet, please don't take him away." As he rode out of our driveway, he waved goodbye saying, "I love you, Mom. See you later!" He had no idea the danger ahead. After he left our home, I cried for weeks missing him, worrying about whether his parents would be able to care for him. He trusted us. He was loved deeply by our family, especially me. He learned about Jesus in our home. He belonged with us! Not by birth, but by choice. It took him so long to trust people—was that all for nothing?

I worked on accepting his return to his birth family, knowing that he would be reunited with his younger brother, who needed him. Several months later, we received a phone call from his mother letting us know he was in the hospital. This tiny boy begged us for a hospital visit following yet another trauma. When we heard, we raced to the hospital to visit him, not knowing what we would find. My foster brother had major injuries and bruising all over his body. He had multiple wounds from his stepfather, who in a rage hit him repeatedly and kicked him in the face. Unsupervised, he crossed a busy street and was struck by a car. He ended up losing a kidney. He was hooked up to machines, bruised and broken. I fainted when I saw him, landing on the floor next to his hospital bed. I couldn't believe how he had been mistreated. No one was protecting him. I couldn't protect him. He was not allowed to return to our home and ended up in multiple placements due to a very broken social service system.

At the time of his recovery my parents had other children placed in their home. Because my little brother needed special care, he ended up shuffled around in the foster care system. Years later I was informed that his father died from cancer and his younger brother took his own life. To this day, I still miss that little boy. His departure, his trauma, and his inability to return to our family was one of the deepest hurts in my backpack.

Accepting losses, especially my foster brother's fate, was not mine to fix. I didn't have control over it. My memories with him brought us joy that no one could take from either of us. Loving him made me a better person, parent, and social worker years later.

There were many moments of pain in my childhood that led me down a path of trying to be perfect, self-deprecating the body that God wanted me to love and honor. I saw the effects of trauma and abuse on many children and their families, and also on me. Despite these hurts, I persisted. All of that negativity seemed to soften when I met the love of my life, my husband, Todd.

HEALTHY LOVE HEALS

"Love is patient, love is kind. It does not envy, it does not boast, it is not proud. It does not dishonor others, it is not self-seeking, it is not easily angered, it keeps no record of wrongs. Love does not delight in evil but rejoices with the truth. It always protects, always trusts, always hopes, always perseveres. Love never fails."

—I CORINTHIANS 13:4-8

I fell in love with my husband, Todd, when I was fourteen years old. I was just a high school freshman and he was a sophomore. We fell in love quickly and deeply. He was cute, funny, kind, and emotionally secure. He loved others naturally and in such a big way. He had all the qualities that I felt I lacked. I was like a magnet to him. I realized early on that he would be my balance. I was shocked that he did not shy away from the chaos of my family, and he gave unconditional support. Finding humor in the dysfunction, he granted me freedom to be exactly who I am. We can't run away from our past. Instead, we must run toward growth. When we have secure roots and wings, we simply fly better.

Todd came from a stable home. His acceptance of everyone was a breath of fresh air from my mistrustful nature. He taught me so much before I turned eighteen that I trusted his instincts more than my own. Despite our fifty-three-day high school breakup (yes, he counted), he stuck by me and loved me, insecurities and all. In so many ways he is the better partner. I am deeply grateful for his faithful love and good sense of humor. He loves playfully, bringing fun to daily life. Without trying, he is exceptionally good at practicing self-care. His love for people leaks into our relationship, forcing me into a life of appreciating the unique qualities that people offer.

I remember the exact day that I knew I would marry him. We were on a date, having dinner at a local family diner. Before being seated, he exited to the restroom. I waited for what seemed to be a long time, he returned to our booth with a gentle smile on his face. He shared that he met a sweet elderly man in the bathroom stall next to him who asked for help. The frail man could not get off the toilet or pull up his pants located by his ankles on the floor. My six-foot-five boyfriend climbed under the bathroom stall, helped this gentleman off the toilet and assisted him with compassion before returning. He apologized for being late and nonchalantly shared this account with me in the most humble and dignified way, reinforcing to me that there are people in this world who see the best in others and will be there for you when you need help, even if they are a total stranger. I loved him so much that day. I still do. His gentle and playful way of solving problems never lets me down.

SERVING PAYS IT FORWARD

"You have two hands. One to help yourself, the second to help others."

—AUDREY HEPBURN

My first job out of college was in a nursing home. I knew immediately that it was the wrong fit because I was miserable. My role focused on accepting residents based on financial status. I craved talking to people, a small piece of my job. However, this not-so-fun job gave me a necessary perspective. A sweet woman named Millie resided there. She was a tiny lady with a bad wig that she wore proudly. One morning I caught her standing in the doorway of my office. She had few visitors and spent most of her days tooling around the facility, brightening the day with her sweet smile and happy disposition. Sensing my unhappiness, she asked me what was wrong. I told her that nothing was wrong, I was simply working on paperwork. She came close to me and placed her aged hand on my arm gently and squeezed. As she looked into my eyes, I remember her saying, "Whatever it is, dear, it won't matter in a hundred years." She smiled, rubbed my arm, and went on her way. Millie's big-picture perspective was a defining moment for me. I realized that I needed to figure out what I wanted to do and make that happen. I had ideas, vision, and an interest in mental health. Life was too short to be unhappy. I could do more. I had to do more.

My next job was on a behavioral health inpatient unit, working with adolescents and assisting the primary therapist. I had a bachelor's degree in clinical psychology and was thrilled to be hired. I knew that mental health was my calling. Within weeks, I began working on both adult and adolescent units. I was assessing and diagnosing patients, counseling, coordinating treatment plans, facilitating groups, doing family sessions, and discharging patients. Although I was hired to work as an assistant, I ended up as a primary mental health counselor due to my ability to pick up the work. I had tireless love for working with hospitalized patients. I soon found myself excited about helping people in the most challenging moments of their lives. This was my niche!

I was newly married, developing relationships with behavioral health professionals in my community. For the next several years I found myself in a sweet spot between being a young mother and having a real career. During this period of my life, I had our first two daughters. I felt like my life couldn't get better. No longer struggling to make bills, I had support from coworkers and close friends who were constantly encouraging me. Life seemed perfect for the very first time.

Due to my husband's growing career, we moved several times, changing jobs and homes to better our position in life. Our daughters, Jordan and Sydney, were the loves of my life. I could see that being a mom was even more fulfilling than my career. Although I carried an internal fear of screwing them up and repeating familial disaster,

I loved parenting. We built a family that centered around Christian love and unity.

Next, I held a position as a community parent educator, hired by a mental health clinic known for in-home family therapy. Working in case management for the W2 program, which assisted families out of poverty and into the workforce, I helped women find jobs, improve their parenting, and learn skills to better manage their lives. Many were low-income, unskilled single parents with significant trauma stories. I diligently mentored them into healthy lifestyle habits. Teaching healthy boundaries, I watched them grow emotionally. I had challenging cases that energized me. The clinic therapists took me under their wings and let me join them in doing in-home family therapy. They educated me on strength-based family therapy using strategic methods to influence change. I gradually developed skills in directing change through clinical techniques. I found my voice and was not afraid to use it.

The owner of the clinic (a professional hero of mine) took time to train me. For my two-year tenure, I learned how to identify systemic premises, watching for patterns in unhealthy family dynamics and applying change tools. I observed skilled clinicians lean into confronting problems with families and having challenging discussions about change. Soaking in knowledge about clinical hypotheses and practicing client engagement skills, I helped clients find resources to improve their functioning. This experience was so powerful.

I had a supervisor who encouraged me to record my thoughts and beliefs. He said, "When you journal, you learn who you are." He explained that writing thoughts and feelings would be one of the best ways to nurture my clinical voice. He saw my potential and encouraged me to return to school. This experience became another defining moment in my backpack, leading me into graduate studies.

When Todd and I discovered that we would be having our third child, I was so excited. He wanted two children, but I wanted more. I knew we could handle more and that our safe little world needed to expand. Raised with mostly sisters, I was relieved that God was blessing us with another little girl. Our third daughter, Payton, was born in March of 1999. She had a rough start with some medical issues, but I knew that God had completed our family when she arrived. Because my pregnancies were rough, I knew that she would be our final child. Accepting this plan, I wanted to be the best mother I could be to our three blessings. I came from a family that was chaotic and needed to use that to raise these girls in a way that created emotional security and consistency. I loved this season of life and wanted to freeze time.

Soon after Payton was born, we moved again—another life transition. Todd was great at bringing new opportunities our way. He had foresight, unwavering faith in the journey, and made everything we did fun, even if it wasn't fun. He left two weeks after she was born to advance his career, as I got the house ready to sell. While home alone with our three little ones, I quit the job I loved and managed the real estate struggle to sell our home. This challenge became a rock star moment for me. I could see how my childhood had prepared me to juggle these responsibilities independently, while Todd began his new work adventure. Looking back, I am amazed how I managed it all. I knew that God was preparing me for more. Another pivotal season of strength in my backpack.

After our move, Todd and I pursued consecutive graduate studies programs, first his, then mine. One at a time, we persevered through the steps it took to accomplish our career goals. I knew that the road would not be easy with small kids. My licensure meant unpaid fieldwork, 3,000 clinical supervised hours, and low-paying jobs. We partnered parenting responsibilities, keeping in step with each other.

During our child-rearing years, we created a friendship with another couple from high school. Our friends had two young daughters around the ages of our girls. Soon after a rekindling connection, we became dear friends. Over the next two decades, we spent vacations together at a shared lake house in the Wisconsin Northwoods. This cabin became a beautiful place to unwind and spend time together on a regular basis. Parenting became easier with the support of another couple going through the same life stages with their daughters. Our cabin getaways gave me the close family experience I sought as a child. It filled my backpack with comradery and clarity for what family means.

During the years of graduate studies, I focused on understanding the clinical frameworks of cognitive behavioral therapy (CBT) and dialectical behavioral therapy (DBT). CBT is about the interplay among thoughts, feelings, and behavior as they intersect with a person's core values. DBT took that a step further, defining specific skills for managing emotions and relationships. Often clients would get stuck in extreme ways of thinking and reacting, which led to my fascination with polarities.

These tools created a path for learning helpful ways of thinking to nurture esteem, create value-focused living, and promote emotional balance. While interning at a county counseling program, I had a generous supervisor who encouraged me to take on challenging cases to expand my skills. He had confidence in my abilities. I began using CBT, exposure therapy, and working with clients of trauma. Soon, I was facilitating groups, working closely with those affected by personality disorders. I saw clients for just three dollars per session.

My husband supported me financially and believed in my dream. I couldn't have done this without him. He nurtured my ideas and trusted me as a parent. I am always trying to make him proud. As a humble, sincere role model for me, he has been the definition of a partner. It's fair to say that I have learned the most from him. When we met in high school, I was insecure, disorganized, and highly resistant to change. He pushed me to talk to people, take calculated risks, and to honor play instead of residing in the insecurity from my childhood. I was madly in love with him as a youth and it has grown over time. Today our love is deep and secure.

After obtaining my master's degree I spent three years in a Christian adolescent residential facility where I was surrounded by God's Word, Christian colleagues, and challenging changes that needed to be made to a vulnerable adolescent residential curriculum.

Finally, I settled into outpatient practice, which became my true love. While working in a state-licensed behavioral health clinic, I found my flow. Nurtured by skilled colleagues, I began my quest to change mental health, developing a consistent clinical practice for the next thirteen years. I had a Christian counseling specialty, working with all ages, couples and families, eventually developing a DBT group program that grew like wildfire. Working with students obtaining licensure, I found a love in mentoring new therapists. I had amazing mentors in my career who inspired me to do the same. I was enjoying a fulfilling clinical practice until one day when I met a CEO of a local company who led me on another career adventure.

When I met Tim Schmidt, the CEO of Delta Defense, he was working through tough losses in his life. After I shared my clinical toolbox with him, he asked me to consider bringing my resources to his fast-growing company. I accepted the position to be the life coach in his organization, where I am honored to use my clinical training to coach employees and nurture the organization's culture. This man is adored by employees and members of his organization.

He is responsible for a culture like none other. He is transparent about his mental health journey of change and promotes well-being in his organization. Unlike most CEOs, he never thinks too much of himself to seek wisdom from others. Both humble and driven, he motivates relentlessly. His leadership philosophy and his "get shit done" attitude has changed my life. He will likely never know the impact he has made in my life. I try to remember to share this gratitude with him as often as possible. Without knowing, he has taught me to fight for what I believe. He repeatedly encouraged me to write this book, and to face my insecurities about my competence to reach my highest potential. This accomplishment now lives in my backpack, creating another avenue for impact.

THE RESILIENT BACKPACK

"If your heart is broken, make art with the pieces."

—SHANE KOYCZAN

Growing up in Two Rivers, Wisconsin, my world was *small*. I remember frequenting the local convenience store buying candy bars with my own money. It was a freedom I loved from a young age. By the fourth grade I was earning my own money. Work became my freedom and curse.

I had a favorite tree in my backyard (called Spidey because of its spiderlike branches) where I read regularly. It became one of my emotionally safe places. The cubby under the stairs was my other safe zone where I would pray, listen to music, and go on imaginary journeys. All my *Charlie's Angels* bubble gum cards lined the walls. These women were tough chicks who kicked ass in pretty outfits, always getting the bad guys and strategically saving the day. They became my superheroes and I needed them. In a strange way they were my imaginary protection against the people in my life who couldn't see me. Music, movies, and books became my outlet for learning. I am grateful for those characters because they empowered me, providing an escape to live vicariously through their fearless adventures.

I struggled with fear of having to see my maternal grandparents, who mistreated my mother and were so emotionally unhealthy. I realized later that their mean-spirited nature was a deep wounded-ness that they either couldn't or didn't want to see. They taught me what *not to do* because of the damage that hurt leaves behind. This insight drove me to surround myself with healthy people. Leaving behind negative people might seem harsh, but it led me to secure relationships that brought peace. Moving on from those who created suffering in my life provided space to examine my pain and see the wisdom that develops from managing it. I intentionally avoided those who regressed my wellness. At first that decision came with guilt, which I had to let go of, removing it from my backpack.

I developed endurance early in life, with my first paid job being at the age of nine. Amy, who was eleven, and I babysat neighbor children (two years old and six weeks old). This challenging summer job was Monday through Friday, ten hours a day. Barely able to take care of ourselves, we were left unsupervised to care for these little ones. Receiving forty-five dollars a week, we considered ourselves young adults.

Likely a result of this experience, we both sustain high expectations of ourselves and others. Amy taught me so much that summer. Together we took on adult responsibilities (illegal by today's standards), juggling more than most young adults of today. We share scary truths that no one would ever believe or understand. Our stories live in her vault, and I visit those with her every now and again in quiet moments we share. I am grateful that at such a young age, I learned how to parent, scrub floors on my hands and knees, do dishes by hand, weed a garden, scour bathrooms, and manage money. The smell of Pine-Sol or Comet quickly transports me to childhood memories. Difficult at the time, this experience afforded me the confidence and skill to manage a family later. This hardship lesson in my backpack allows me to juggle multiple responsibilities.

By the time I was twelve, I was working Friday and Saturday nights at a local bar that my father managed. I was cleaning my grandmother's salon on Saturday mornings with my mother by my side and babysitting in the neighborhood every opportunity available.

When my girls were young, they spent their summer days playing freely. My life had adult responsibilities that other children didn't experience. I enjoyed earning my own money to buy the name-brand items that I thought would help me blend in with my peers. I just wanted to be like everyone else. Little did I know that fitting in did not promote belonging but led to more insecurity. This internal battle was essential to my growth, helping me eventually accept and embrace my individuality. Although difficult at the time, it gave me the strength to carry heavy loads in my backpack, nurturing resilience. This early "adulting" developed humility and a tenacious work ethic, preparing me for parenthood and building distress tolerance skills.

Over time, God led me to incredible people who helped heal my heart, while distancing me from others who were toxic. I can see on the outside of my pain that He was with me the entire time. I never needed that control to begin with.

Without emotional pain, I would not hold on to the values that are dear to me.

Because of the hurt, I am hardworking, faithful, and growth driven.

Because of the hurt, I persevere well.

Because of the hurt, I know how to heal in tough circumstances.

Because of the hurt, I am fearless in my efforts to help others.

Because of the hurt, I rely on God and the lessons He gives to make me better.

Because of the hurt, I love deeply and compassionately.

Resilience is our ability to bounce back from pain, applying the lessons that come from those moments. What has your hurt taught you? How has it made you resilient? Write down your list of hurts, identifying what each challenge has taught you. Review this every day. It strengthens the way you carry your load.

Pay attention to your resilience. It helps. A lot.

FOR YOUR BACKPACK

The meaning you assign to your experience affects how you carry your backpack. Carry it with resilience, learning lessons for growth.

YOUR BACKPACK

"I praise you because I am fearfully and wonderfully made."

—PSALM 139:14

5 RULES FOR YOUR BACKPACK

Let's talk about your backpack. Learning how to focus on what you have control over is not always easy. Your perspective comes from your experience, impacting how you see yourself and others.

Let's review:

- Your backpack is about your perception (thoughts, feelings, needs, and choices) in any given situation, based on your experience.
- Others do not have to agree or share your view. The position they take is about their experience, not yours.
- How you view the experiences in your life shapes your relationship with self and others.
- Those who take the time to make connections between their past and present choices understand themselves on a deeper level. This leads to connections with others regarding their personal truths.

- The process of unpacking your backpack (understanding why you think and react as you do) defines meaning and personal strength.
- Understanding how you view stress and deal with hurt impacts the weight and how you carry your backpack and interact with others.

Here are a few rules that guide how you implement this philosophy in your life.

RULE 1
Know Your Backpack

In order to understand your backpack (your boundaries associated with your experience), you need peace with your past hurts, clear understanding of the values that guide your present, and consistently followed habits aligned with goals for your future.

Your backpack holds beliefs defined by your *past* that impact your current emotional struggles. Insight occurs when you assess how negative past events trigger your emotionality. By identifying the strengths and lessons gained from positive and negative life events, your perspective expands. To be emotionally well, you must accept the past, seeing strength that resulted from your past. Making connections to memories that have shaped your perspective assists you in understanding the impact of these events. Do you have hurts from your past that you need to work through and let go of? Who were the instrumental people negatively affecting your emotions? What emotional triggers resulted from your negative experiences? Journaling this helps you identify when these hurts get triggered by others around you.

Tune into your defensive moments. These reflection questions will create understanding in the moment of your triggered reaction.

- Where in your past might this triggered reaction originate from? Define moments from your past that led to the feeling, examining the connection between past and present emotions.
- What part of this situation belongs to you and what belongs to another?
- What could this moment be teaching you? Is there a lesson in it?
- What options or solutions bring alignment with your values?

By connecting your "in the moment" reaction to events from your past, you can direct your mind to let go of the old habit, updating your mindset to what you need now.

Our habits are so ingrained that it can become "normal" to be in negative emotional frequencies. In triggered reactions, our brain tells us that it is someone else's problem, rather than seeing it as our own habit response that needs to change. This critical moment is the pathway to understanding what bothered you about the situation and why, giving you an opportunity to intentionally direct your behavior in a purposeful way.

When upset, it is easy to react or resist to control the situation. You don't need to do either. Reacting often leads to either pleasing or blaming others. Resisting results in avoidance of solving the problem. The solution lies within you. With a peaceful attitude, you can share your needs openly and directly. This emotional boundary process involves calmly asking questions first, listening to understand. Too often we get stuck on needing agreement rather than understanding.

Internal disharmony is the test of your emotional skill level. Your self-talk in any given difficulty can connect you to "the whys" of your feelings. By slowing down, you can reflect on how you think and feel. Understanding is necessary in communicating from your best voice. By slowing down the process, talking it through in your mind, you stop the need to block or overthink, which drains your energy tank. It also prevents the damage caused by your bad mood, which spills onto others negatively when you vent frustrations.

Your negativity comes from insecurity and fear. It is not easy to notice this in the moment. Our loved ones often point this out before we see it in ourselves. It takes time to retrain the brain to notice our blind spots, resetting the emotion before communicating. We quickly become self-concerned as we listen to the negative thoughts and feelings that accompany our triggers. As you notice and direct your thoughts, you practice identifying the solution most helpful for you. Deciding that your experience is yours and that it doesn't have to be liked by others is a backpack revelation.

Your backpack contains your *present*. When you are emotionally healthy, your values guide your decisions. Clearly defining your values helps you to be consistent with your best-self choices. They are your guide in the most difficult circumstances. Write out your values, defining how they lead you. Identify when you are not congruent with your values. This reflection helps you separate triggered moments from your intentional self.

When emotionality occurs, keeping your focus on the present moment reinforces the backpack principle that keeps your boundaries consistent. Observing your emotions neutrally (without negative energy) encourages alignment. When you avoid or attach to a strong emotion, you lose alignment. Focusing on what you can do to be calm, rather than on the trigger, keeps you in your present moment. Define your boundaries by journaling what belongs to you and what belongs to others in situations that bother you.

Your backpack contains your potential *future* self. Ask yourself:

What are my goals in this situation? What choices keep my alignment with my big-picture needs? How will I execute my resolve skillfully in my best self?

Your backpack is uniquely yours. Decorate it with your signature style. Be who you are, without excuse or apology. Enjoy your uniqueness, embracing the process of managing your faults and pushing the limits on your needed growth. Visualize for a moment what your backpack looks like based on your individual personality. This exercise reminds you that your choices on this hike belong to you.

Will you choose to take judgment out of your backpack? It will make a difference if you do. Judgment shows up when you are noticing the flaws of others or when you are in self-directed criticism. Observing flaws is helpful to your growth. Focusing on them is not. Knowing your backpack is being clear about who you are, both strengths and weaknesses. It incorporates accountability and awareness about what you need from others. Focusing on you decreases defenses about the perception and opinions of others. When you worry about what others think and feel, you stop moving forward. A growth mindset is key to being a healthy you.

RULE 2
Stop Comparing Your Backpack

We spend way too much time comparing ourselves to others. Think of the many ways you do this. Do you compare your physical appearance, home, relationships, children, finances, happiness, and worth with others? Doing this is dangerous because we know very little about the big-picture life of others. This common error produces unnecessary emotion. Comparison thoughts are often inaccurate and seldom give us the outcome we want. Emotions about what others have is unproductive. Catch yourself in this dance of comparison, shifting your attention from a paradigm of scarcity to abundance. Notice what you have, not what you don't. When worry about not having or being enough lives in your mind, you miss out on your blessings.

Your backpack is beautiful, even if it is heavy, worn out, or unlike that of others. Your history gives you wisdom and lessons for growth. You can see your strengths and weaknesses without comparing or living for others. Patterned criticism against the self and others is poison to your soul. It results in mirroring how others feel and assigning worth based on their perception or feelings, rather than your own. Comparison does not produce peace. It nurtures insecurity.

Eli was a client of mine years ago who came from a large family. He was a middle child of six children with successful older and younger siblings. When he started his therapy, he was convinced he had imposter syndrome. Imposter syndrome is an internalized pattern of doubting your skills and abilities in fear that someone will find out that you are not as capable as they think you are. This faulty belief fuels insecurities, promoting comparison, make you feel like you can never measure up. Eli was stuck in this paradigm. He took longer to get through college, struggled with getting an initial professional job, and moved home with his parents after college. His siblings were quickly successful and would comment negatively to him that he was failing according to their family standards. He later met his wife and had a son but continued to compare himself to other colleagues, family members, and friends who were "more" successful than him.

We discussed the importance of not comparing himself to others who had different experiences than he did. Eli had medical issues that slowed down his timeline and required more self-care. As he learned to embrace his life story, he started focusing on personal wins, accepting his worth rather than comparing to others. His confidence grew with this boundary in place, letting go of his "not good enough" identity. He retrained his negative self-talk to accept himself and be happy.

RULE 3
Clean Out Your Backpack Regularly

By slowing down and reflecting on your intention regularly, you keep your emotional backpack organized. Through consistent reflection, you will learn to practice letting go of things out of your control that provide emotional stress. This might be something said that hurt your feelings or a situation that didn't turn out the way you hoped. By contemplating daily lessons of growth, your muscles for carrying your backpack get stronger with practice. Over time, you build a secure voice that is helpful in communicating your needs with others.

Examine the items in your backpack that do not belong to you or need to be removed. When you have learned what past mistakes have taught you, remove them. Some thoughts, feelings, beliefs, and messages come from people in your past. Others belong to people you are trying to impress or please. Finally, some come from fear, unresolved anger, or old hurts. Let these things go. Don't let the labels or judgments of others live in your backpack. Notice how the weight of those items has made you strong. Let go because you don't need to carry those anymore. Learn the lessons of your past so you can walk forward.

Every year I go through my closet and clean it out. I donate or discard items I don't need, reorganizing the space. We can do this type of cleaning with our emotional life too. Let go of the thoughts you don't want. Make peace with old hurts. Update your mindset. Set new goals. When we do this regularly, we grow into our best self.

Decide to examine your brain's worry mode. You can tell yourself that thinking about "the what ifs" makes you prepared for what is ahead. But, is that true? Most of the things we worry about never happen. And if they do, you will figure it out. When you notice your pattern of worry, direct your mind to a more productive focus in your present moment. Observe that negative moment like a gust of wind. Notice it, but don't fear or chase it. Be neutrally aware of it as you hike. If you put worry in your backpack it is heavy and it creates fatigue. Choose not to carry it. Think of it as wind from this point forward, noticing it as it passes by you.

Doing a daily reflection can start or end each day with a purposeful intention. Discard the messages that you no longer need to carry around with you. Ask yourself: what can I do *more of* and *less of* today to make me better than yesterday? If you did this exercise daily, your backpack would stay organized.

RULE 4
Set Down Your Backpack When You Are Tired

Resetting emotionally is necessary to keep balance. Stress is unavoidable; we all have it and struggle with it. In order to be competent humans, we need stress. Fighting it is futile. Struggling keeps us humble so our ego does not make us arrogant know-it-alls. Life is challenging and unpredictable. Self-care fills your emotional bucket, allowing you to handle problems that drain your energy. Slowing down to reset is how you set down your backpack. Self-care is about focusing your energy on meaningful activities that rejuvenate the fatigue caused by stress.

Consider the following energy-producing activities:

- Exercising
- Reading
- Journaling growth
- Enjoying the outdoors
- Spending time with positive loved ones
- Engaging in creative activities or hobbies
- Cooking
- Gardening

Taking breaks to recharge your batteries helps you get more done in the big picture. Identify your emotional reset activities that refuel your hike when negativity weighs down your backpack.

RULE 5
Wear Your Backpack without Complaining

As you practice moving forward, challenge yourself to think helpfully. By accepting discomfort for the benefit of growth, you will find new paths that lead to wisdom. The circumstances that create emotion are opportunities for growth. Whether you are in boredom, loneliness, apathy, or frustration, the emotion is your teacher. When you discover the lesson of what you need to do, it no longer controls you. This learning reduces complaining. Complaining leads to misery, not peace.

We spend a great deal of time doing tasks to cross things off a list, rather than doing them in enjoyment. When we learn to love any task (even boring activities), we wear our backpack more securely and the hike is more satisfying.

We complain that there is not enough time because we have so much to do. As a culture, we thrive on being busy, but then grumble because we don't have time to do the things we want to do. We avoid doing the things that we don't like, procrastinating. Is it possible to embrace that which is uninteresting if we haven't liked it before? It is like enjoying food you didn't care for as a child. You can appreciate any activity, even getting up in the morning. Learning to enjoy household chores or managing your finances with the right attitude creates energy. By seeing challenges as problem-solving experiments, you teach yourself to think skillfully as you perform these habits. Moving through the day's events can be mindless. Intention in these moments shifts the mind to enjoying even simple tasks.

What activities of daily life would you like to enjoy more? What will you do to challenge your mindset around these moments? Will you listen to music, think about your loved ones, or maybe practice being present?

Happiness does not come from what we have or what we get. It involves keeping our alignment, serving others with our unique gifts. Practicing this mindset leads to carrying our burdens without complaining. Let's collectively decide to pivot away from complaining because it leads to division. The key is to observe negative situations, without giving energy to them, carrying simply what belongs to you in the best way you know how. The road can be strenuous at times, but your mindset along the way is your choice. Choose a helpful one. See the growth that results.

HIKING WITH YOUR BACKPACK

"Your journey will still be difficult, but the map shouldn't be. Knowing where you're going, how to get there, and how to tell where you are right now should be the easy part!"

—BRIAN S. HOLMES

In many ways, our emotional journey replicates the physical hikes we take. If you decided to go hiking, there are steps you would likely take to make sure you are prepared. You prepare your backpack beforehand. If it is a long journey you might bring food and water, GPS, a trail map, and other necessary supplies. If you are a skilled hiker, you would set aside time to look at the trail assessing how strenuous it might be and what you would need. You would dress appropriately for the weather conditions and prepare ahead of time.

Our well-being works similarly. One of my favorite quotes by Joyce Sunada states, "If you don't take time for your wellness, you will be forced to take time for your illness." This is what wellness prevention and preparation are all about. What are you doing to be intentionally well physically, emotionally, socially, and spiritually? Your habits do not need to be a result of circumstances, but rather choice.

If I am headed into a difficult moment or season of life, can I do things that help the process go smoother? Absolutely. For example, if I am suffering a loss, I need to know what grief can do to my emotional and physical functioning. This is part of the preparation phase; I observe how I am handling the loss. This prevention method encourages openly talking about feelings associated with the loss and working through grief stages, rather than carrying it as deficiency or avoiding it because it simply hurts too much. Preparing for emotional struggles won't stop the hurt. It normalizes human functioning and helps in the acceptance of the hurt as you move through it over time.

What helps you prepare for your hurts? Reading helps. Journaling helps. Openly talking about how you feel helps. Meaningful activities help. Knowing the warning signs of disordered habits leads toward healing and pain-related growth.

When you intentionally manage your load without focusing on the problem itself, you build endurance. When you do that emotionally by confronting challenging situations head-on, you gain an emotional workout that builds confidence and emotional stamina.

For example, if I am going to confront a friend who frequently gossips about another friend, this is a tough situation. If I am in her backpack, I might make excuses for her or join in because of my need to people please. If I am focused on my backpack solely, I would ask questions about how she is feeling, bringing attention to our shared values in a nonjudgmental way. My focus must be on my alignment because it belongs to me. This may be an emotional workout because of the preparation time in my mind to confront this skillfully, but worth the effort.

Hiking can be a way of seeing the beauty all around us. Can you imagine going for a hike and never looking around at the scenery? The beauty of the sky and plants around you is critical to the hike. On rare occasions you might see wildlife or notice a special item along the path that is unique. Our senses are filled when we are outdoors exploring. This happens when we are exploring inside of ourselves too! The more you work on understanding and being who you are, the more satisfying the experience.

I was on a hike years ago with close friends. Although not an avid hiker, I was with athletic women who had all the right supplies and stamina for the hike. I hadn't prepared at all. My shoes were new and gave me blisters. I hadn't done any training beforehand to get in shape. The first time I viewed the trail map was right before we left. When you aren't prepared, problems often occur. My experience taught me to ask questions and better prepare for the next one. This strenuous hike taught me to confront my resistance to exercise and push through the discomfort. The challenges you choose to learn from along life's way are your best hikes.

I struggled when I compared myself to my friends who were skillful hikers, not recognizing my beginner status in this new skill. My value of determination helped me persist until the end of this long hike. In the big picture, I knew I could do it, even unprepared. We are not prepared for every struggle we face. But our mindset allows us to get through it if we understand clearly what belongs to us. Your values serve as your compass, guiding you on the tough hikes. Enjoy the ones that challenge you and make you a better hiker. You become emotionally athletic through the practice.

Secure your backpack. No matter how difficult the hike, you can do it. Don't turn back. The past is meant to teach, not to torture you. Let the moments along the way provide lessons for the future. Challenging moments make us who we are, preparing us for more.

10 LESSONS FOR YOUR BACKPACK

"Lessons in life will be repeated until they are learned."

—FRANK SONNENBERG

LESSON 1
Anxiety, the Faulty Fuse

Anxiety is a worldwide phenomenon. We call it "stress" to reduce the stigma, but it is anxiety. Anxiety shows up in negative thoughts and strong emotion. Do any of the following patterns sound like you?

- "I am not good enough" or other high-insecurity thoughts
- The pattern of shifting back and forth between tense/high-

energy moments that lead to low energy/shutting down in fatigue

- Body pain, gastrointestinal issues, headaches, inflammation, immune suppression, sweating, nausea, heart palpitations, trembling, or hypervigilance
- Patterns of needing to cope through escape behaviors (food, substances, spending, electronics, sleep, work, or activities that prevent us from thinking about things that bother us) to avoid negative thoughts or feelings
- Racing thoughts and racing adrenaline in the body
- Moodiness, particularly irritability, restlessness, high frustration, worry, apathy, sadness, and loud emotion
- Overreacting internally or externally, leading to negative self-talk and conflict
- Unhealthy beliefs about yourself and/or others
- Feeling chronically overwhelmed, needing to be busy to avoid this feeling

Anxiety is different for each person. As a result, many do not recognize the signs. Old stigma myths picture anxiety as weakness or brokenness in one's character. This view is simply not true. Anxiety brings strengths that make people exceptional. Those with anxiety often have high empathy, compassion, and emotional awareness. When you are both aware of it and skilled at regulating it, anxiety becomes your superpower. Do not hide it, give it power to embarrass you, or use it as a weapon or excuse.

I have terrible allergies. I have never thought that this trait made me less worthy than someone without allergies. The same is true for anxiety, depression, or any other issue. When conditions are managed skillfully, they can be useful. We get what we get. It is our responsibility to understand it and regulate it to our best ability.

Take time to understand your body's reaction to your unique stress triggers. How does this impact your beliefs about yourself and others? Do your behavioral habits support wellness or misery? Your energy and personal satisfaction come from how you manage your way through difficult moments.

When I started understanding adrenal balance, my ability to provide a helping map for others changed. Early in my field of study, I had learned that exercise and relaxation were helpful to the body and mind, but I didn't know why. When I discovered how the brain increases cortisol (the stress hormone) and adrenaline in acute stress moments, I was struck by how important this education was to clients who struggle with anxiety and depression.

In a workshop, an instructor drew a chart that demonstrated optimal brain balance as it relates to internal stress. She went on to share that negative events from the past can trigger the brain to periods of intense emotion. This zone of emotional functioning, called hyperarousal, creates intense surges of adrenaline that eventually result in lower disengaged functioning and fatigue, called hypoarousal. These internal functioning zones are connected to cortisol levels that activate adrenal glands and flood the body's energy system moving it from too much energy to not enough energy. With repeated triggers, the brain develops a pattern of functioning from high stress to emotional numbing. This fight or flight pattern is a part of the brain's amygdala, creating emotional urgency that we need for an actual crisis. When this occurs in normal day-to-day activities, it ends up being a *faulty fuse* that gets tripped, producing anxiety.

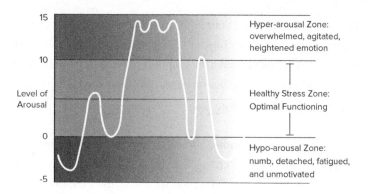

Window of Tolerance, adapted from Ogden et al., 2006;
Siegal, 1999; and Van der Hart et al.,2006.

I refer to this process with my clients as the brain's faulty fuse box. It reminds me of blow-drying my hair in my childhood home. After just a few minutes of use, the outlet would suddenly stop working. I remember having to run down to the basement fuse box to find the bathroom breaker and flip the switch so that the outlet would work again. If you look at emotional triggers like a faulty fuse box that requires a "flip of the switch," you will learn to notice your miswired brain moment. It requires internal observation of the triggered event, leading to your reaction (the blowing of the outlet) and what you do to "flip the switch" to regain balance (your intentional choice to reset your response). We can address the issue internally by changing our energy and shifting the mind.

If I hadn't understood what was happening, I would have thought that the outlet didn't work. Today most outlets have reset buttons that resolve electrical failures. You can learn to reset when your emotional outlet does not work properly. By observing triggered responses in your body, you can find your way back to your healthy stress zone, resetting intention with your body, mind, and behavior.

Your brain and body need to be understood in order to manage your internal system properly.

Negative emotional habits require a process of slowing down, observing, and readjusting the moment in order to make a conscious decision. For example, if a person says something to you that ignites a strong reaction, observe the way this trigger affects you. If you obsessively circle the issue over and over, you will become fatigued from that emotional stress. Similarly, if you spend emotional energy resisting the thoughts and feelings from the trigger, you will have a similar result.

Your impulse inside may be to "keep busy" to block the unwanted feelings, which diminishes your emotional presence. Being aware of your patterned habits provides insight about when to flip your internal reset switch. When you realize that you have been triggered, consciously directing your body and thoughts into balance, realignment occurs. This practice over time can reset the faulty fuse and restore balance. Awareness of the fight or flight mode is the first step. Slowing down the body and thoughts is the second step. Intentionally directing the mind to focus on what you have control over is the final step in the reset process. Once reinforced systematically, the brain learns to repair the faulty fuse pattern and anxiety no longer wins.

You have the power to flip the switch inside to help your body and brain work better when this fight or flight adrenal surge takes over. The brain's crisis mode function is helpful when you are in true crisis. It is not meant for stress in daily life. Let's keep that alarm just for crises!

LESSON 2

Intention and Time Coping Partners

There are two specific tools I recommend for people to assess their coping skills during stress. They are:

1. Examining the *intention* of your choice.
2. Assessing the amount of *time* engaged in the coping skill.

Ask yourself this question: when I am stressed, what are the ways that I deal with my stress?

Here are some ways people cope:

- Emotional eating or restricting eating
- Substances—alcohol, marijuana, caffeine, nicotine, or hard drugs
- Spending money
- Sexual thoughts or behaviors
- Electronics—computer, video games, phone time, television, or social media
- Preoccupation in the lives of others
- Extreme forms of self-care, exercise, or dietary restrictions
- Obsessive and compulsive behaviors
- Shutting down—getting lost in your head
- Being compulsively busy to avoid the stress
- Excessive sleep or couch time
- Isolation—avoiding people and social situations

Identify for yourself if you have any of these patterns. In what situations do you observe yourself engaging in these unhelpful habits? When you notice it, you can change it.

Remember, your stories create your reality. Until you take the time to observe, your thoughts become your perception of truth. For example, you might justify gossip because a coworker was rude first. It's easy to convince yourself that a lost-temper parenting moment is healthy because you are teaching values in tough love. You make excuses for unhelpful self-care patterns and procrastinating on goals. Inconsistency with exercise is due to fatigue or not feeling well. Convenience eating is because of time constraints. Drinking too much is because of work stress justifying that "I deserve to have a little fun, right?" You hide your true feelings because others will not understand or listen. You judge others because they are doing things that are "wrong." Take a moment to notice the stories that justify your negative coping habits. You believe these stories as truth until you choose to challenge your mindset to think constructively.

Holly, how do I know if my coping skills are healthy? I have been asked this question many times. Working through stress is different than coping with it. Examining intention is necessary to assessing your behavior. By questioning whether you are seeing things from a healthy perspective, you can begin to observe the difference between your initial response to a situation and your intended choice. Your behavior can be led by your peaceful moral compass if you direct it clearly.

If you have a difficult family member who ends up being a "time vampire" in your life, how do you know if you are handling this relationship in the right way? What if you are working long hours at work and lack the time to deal with your physical health? What if you and your partner aren't connecting well? What if your children are doing things that you morally stand against? How do you know if you are doing the right things to manage difficult circumstances? Examine your intention. Ask yourself this question: what am I trying to accomplish in this situation and how will I direct my way through it productively?

It's easy to get into a so-called *normal* pattern that feels comfortable but doesn't resolve the issue. If you are unhappy in your marriage and feel depressed, you might see a mental health provider who prescribes medication to treat your depression. What if the real issue is the way you think about and interact with your partner? In that scenario, medication will not resolve your issue.

Treating the core issue solves the dysfunction. Our medical resources for clinical depression have helped many people with serious mental health disorders and this is essential. In those circumstances, the primary problem may be biogenetic brain imbalance, and medication is a helpful option or component of the solution. But in situational problems, addressing the core issue is resolving the marital differences. This requires leaning into uncomfortable discussions repeatedly and creating a healthy skills plan, pressing on until both partners have peaceful resolve. Systematically working on changing the unhealthy habits contaminating the relationship will bring resolve. Peaceful resolution is not about blame, judgment, or making the other person happy. When you are clear about what you have control over and what you don't (your backpack), this process is simplified. Although we often are blind in the moment of frustration, we have control over how we choose to resolve any dilemma.

Going deeper, I encourage you to assess whatever concern you have against these two constructs: *intention* and *time*. If your intention is driven by emotion (fear, worry, anger, apathy, boredom, loneliness, or a general avoidance of dealing with the situation because it is difficult), it is not the right intention. When we avoid or react to negative life situations because they make us uncomfortable, we are not solving our problems. The end result will be more of the same.

On the other hand, if you are making the choice because you have carefully examined options available to you and the reasons are aligned with your values, it is likely to bring on a peaceful outcome. Even if others do not agree or like it, the intention in your choice needs to be clear to you. This is operating skillfully from your backpack.

For example, if you are working sixty-plus hours a week at work, this could be healthy or unhealthy based on your intention. If you are putting in extra time temporarily for a big-picture cause, knowing that you will slow down for self-care after the need fades, working long hours could pay off. However, if your motivation is unhealthy (for others to see you as hardworking, avoiding stress at home, competing with another coworker, endlessly seeking more money), your intentions will be driven by emotion and your body will produce higher levels of the stress hormone to carry in your backpack. Intention matters.

Let's say you set a goal to lose weight. If your intention is driven by vanity in order to look good or to impress others around you, the intention is unhealthy. If your intention is to have good health, it is core connected. The behavior in either circumstance could be the same, but the intention is not. One choice leads to anxiety, the other to peace. This process can be utilized for any coping skill.

If I tell myself that I am going to be consistent in finishing a project, but then blame my inconsistency on recent circumstances, I alter my mindset to justify my lack of accountability. Blame and excuses alleviate the discomfort from owning poor follow-through, which feels better in that moment.

The pattern of distorting reality begins early in life. It begins in childhood when we blame others for not giving us our way. Blame shifts our focus from our own mistakes to someone or something else, blocking intention. Decide to watch for your excuses to be off track. You can notice them like signs on the street. When you slow down your thoughts enough to catch yourself in that moment of excuse, you can decide on your intention. Watch what happens when you practice this skill. It is exciting.

The second tool for examining your coping skills is time. The time element works similarly to intention. If you assess your habit based on frequency and intensity, you will be able to see if it is balanced. Check for binary thinking accompanying all-or-nothing patterns. The frequency and intensity of your coping choices are indicators of imbalance. Anytime you are in all-or-nothing extremes, you are likely outside the healthy regulation zone.

Take cleaning, for example. Cleaning is a responsible choice. But what if it consumes hours every day and is obsessional? This control behavior, which produces a good outcome, can be examined by the amount of time that you are giving it each day. This can be true of other choices that seem healthy or positive. Assess how much energy you are giving to daily activities.

Consider these areas:

- Work
- Food
- Alcohol
- Spending
- Exercise
- Sleep
- Digital devices
- Thinking

There is a balance zone in how much time is healthy for any activity.

| ① | ⋯ | ② | ⋯ | ③ | ⋯ | ④ | ⋯ | ⑤ | ⋯ | ⑥ | ⋯ | ⑦ | ⋯ | ⑧ | ⋯ | ⑨ | ⋯ | ⑩ |

Always ⋯⋯⋯⋯⋯⋯ *Sometimes* ⋯⋯⋯⋯⋯ *Never*

Assess time using this spectrum with always and never on the ends of the continuum. Where are you on that continuum with your unhealthy habits? Carefully examine your time priorities. When do you fall into your extreme habits? By spotting your "all-or-nothing" moments you can set personal boundaries with the amount of time that you choose to give to any activity in question. Doing a priority time log helps you accurately see how you spend your downtime in emotion-numbing activities. Pursuing balance with time and intention will allow you to see when you are stuck in unhelpful habits. Stretch your skills to find middle ground patterns.

Accurately appraising intention and time can create forward movement to practicing new habits. It's a way to stop worrying about what you "should" do to please others. Instead, it pivots direction toward what you do have control over—yourself. Focus on *your* backpack.

Assess your coping choices with intention and time. Stop living in the all-or-nothing cycle. Begin the practice of doing things in a new way. The process of growth is a mindful walk. Keep intention and time tools in your backpack from here forward.

LESSON 3
Connect Before Correct

One of the mistakes I notice people make is sharing their opinions too quickly. Sometimes this happens because we are uncomfortable hearing about problems and want to give a quick solution. Without thinking, we share opinions as gospel truth, not realizing the limited view, based on our backpacks. When relationships become comfortable over time, it is easy to get in a pattern of talking without considering the feelings of others. I believe it is why we are more careful at work than in our personal relationships. Our loved ones deserve the best of us, not our end-of-the-day emotional leftovers.

Connecting in closeness means taking the time to understand how another views a problem. This connecting before correcting approach is empathic communication. When you take time to connect first, keeping energy safe and warm, while verbalizing positive intention, you communicate with skill. Connecting first allows you to address feelings before making corrections through clear boundaries.

One of the tools I have shared for decades has been the LUV first (listen, understand, validate) method. When you need to set a boundary, this three-step tool is useful:

1. *Listen* attentively before responding.
2. Use *understanding* words.
3. *Validate* feelings expressed.

When you LUV first, you will have greater connection to share your perspective. This slows the communication process down; there is no interruption or negative energy getting in the way. This tool will help you connect before you share a boundary from your backpack. It will reduce your empathy failure moments!

LESSON 4
Your Big Bad Hairy Ego

I recall a moment at work where a colleague of mine noticed one of my less than pleasurable moods. I don't recall what was bothering me, but I can tell you that I was not my typical jolly self. Across the lunch table, he commented, "*You know, Holly, you are not that big of a deal.*" I chuckled inside, knowing with certainty that his comment was not meant to offend, but to bring insight. It became another defining backpack moment. As a therapist I was teaching others to be more self-aware, while struggling to apply it in a benign moment. I was in my blind spot. What others say and do is not about us. It comes from what they carry in their backpack, based on their experiences.

When we get caught up in an emotional spiral of negative thoughts, we make ourselves a big deal. Perspective is about seeing the big picture. Ego is about seeing how it affects "me" in a moment of time. This phrase became a mantra in my backpack that frequently shifted my mood when impacted by negative thoughts. I watched for moments when I could use it to retrain a mindset of self-concern. Feelings are useful in the development of insight. They are not the drivers of choice, but part of personal awareness. The quicker we can spot our ego, the better we are able to switch gears and get back on track. Awareness of how you are feeling is necessary. But it means little without regulation.

Today there are endless books on mindfulness and intention that address the concept of the ego. I remember first reading about the ego in college from the work of Sigmund Freud, the founder of psychology back in the late nineteenth century. The ego, according to Freud, is our "want center" of human experience. It pulls us into self-pity and frustration when we don't get our way. This "wanting what we desire" is often at the core of negative moods. In this self-focused mindset, it's easy to notice what we lack rather than what we have. When we have more, we want more. If we don't get what we want, we quickly develop our reason for why we are unhappy, which usually results in blame.

As this pattern continues, our mind compares ourselves to others, feeling jealous or judgmental about the choices of other people. Notice when your ego surfaces in these moments of dissatisfaction. This is the moment we are frustrated or annoyed with another. When this occurs for you, say to yourself, "No thank you, ego. I am not that big of a deal."

The struggle with ego begins early in life. Toddlers want the toy that another child found. This pattern of noticing what others have occurs throughout the life span, nurturing competition in multiple arenas (academia, fashion, athletics, financial living, family life, etc.). It holds space in social media to report what we have, often taking away from our unique experience. Although you want it, you don't need validation by others. Whether others like what you do doesn't matter. Choose to celebrate the successes of others authentically. Don't let the fear of being good enough rise up and create anxiety.

Inferiority thinking is judgment pointed at self. This type of judgment sees your experience as having less opportunity, experience, or value than others. When inferiority thinking drives behavior, you become a victim of circumstances, nurturing a depressed mood. This loop of ruminating on what you lack becomes a pattern that separates you from others, nurturing negativity. When in victim thinking, you distort reality by seeing the successes of others as a result of luck, circumstances, or greed. When below optimal functioning, you might seek things that numb insecure feelings and provide pleasure. This inferiority happens when you perceive injustice or didn't get what you felt entitled to.

We are uniquely ourselves; it does not make sense to compare our experience to another's. We don't need to compete with anyone. Competition needs to be with ourselves, striving for progress in our best self each day. None of us need this inferiority message in our backpack.

Similarly, superiority thinking is pointed at others. When others do things that are unhelpful, it is easy to see your perspective as better. When you label others, you inflate your perspective or truth. When you apply the backpack philosophy, you stop attaching to or resisting what others are doing. This frees you from the judgment that creates your hypocrisy. You are not better or worse than anyone else. Neither am I. We simply carry our backpack differently because of the items in it. Security is about neutrally understanding this without judgment.

When my girls ran cross-country in high school, each week they tried to beat their personal running record. I cautioned them not to compare their running to anyone else's, only to their own last run. What if we did this in life? Let's decide to stop comparing ourselves to others. Competition does not need to drive you. Your esteem is not about anyone other than you. With this boundary lesson, reaching your next forward place can be your new norm.

What does it mean to be emotionally secure? Security is about operating from *peace* and *patience*, without defensiveness. It is experienced when you can access your peaceful self in a challenging moment. By keeping alignment with your values as your guide to solutions, your defensive behavior diminishes.

Watch for these moments:

- Shutting down or withdrawing fully in conversation
- Feeling attacked or judged
- Raising your voice/taking a negative tone
- Complaining or venting (internally or with others)

- Avoiding a situation that needs to be addressed
- Ruminating on the negative
- Changing the subject
- Walking on eggshells
- Being sarcastic, rude, or passive-aggressive

You can use your secure voice in any situation. By observing *what*, *how*, and *why* you do what you do, you practice secure living. Don't give power to your ego. Instead take time to be secure in your perspective before you open your mouth. Self-control is key to managing your big bad hairy ego.

I believe the defensiveness that comes from fear is at the core of any "ism" in our world. It's at the core of division. Insecurity leads to personal unhappiness. It creates relationship, organizational, and political division. Division separates people. Standing for a cause can be peaceful. When it is not, the gap between sides grows bigger. When we decide to address this, we abandon self-righteousness and taking on peaceful optimism. Let's stop the madness of being better or worse than others, practicing peace and patience to understand the experience of others and what they carry. Secure thinking drives connection, nurturing trust.

Observing the impulse to judge yourself (inferiority) or others (superiority) leads to contentment. I believe that it is why spiritual connection is so important. When we pay attention to meaning apart from our narrow experience, a greater purpose develops. We lack insight to change ourselves when misery is about others. Ego clouds big-picture judgment, leading to a cycle of complaining and negativity.

Acceptance of the present moment leads to peace in a frustrating moment. How we direct our thoughts is something we have control over as healthy humans. When our internal dialogue is productive, particularly in moments of emotional triggers, we develop a mind muscle that extinguishes personal negativity.

The secure mind celebrates others. When you put the best spin on the misfortunes of others, you accept that they are doing the best they can with what they know. Emotional security strives to see the efforts of those around you without worrying about how it impacts you. This allows you to enjoy people fully for their strengths. In the same realm it sees the best in self, accurately appraising both strengths and weaknesses. When I started to do this, my life changed. I am not that big of a deal. You are not a big deal either. Carry your backpack securely, friend.

LESSON 5
The 4 Ps–Past, Present, Potential, and Purpose

Your backpack contains your past, present, potential, and purpose. You are responsible for managing all four parts. This makes therapy helpful—it is a process of understanding how your past impacts your present and future potential.

Ask yourself these questions:

1. *Past:* What are the positive and negative life events that have shaped your personality? What negative patterns come from your past? As you reflect, assign purposeful meaning to negative events, no longer giving them control over you. Make a list of resentments you choose to let go of, freeing you from internal negativity that triggers pain. It is time to stop looking back on the roads of your past. *"Why" something happens is never more important than what you do with it.* Once you are clear with how your past hurts have made you wiser, you no longer need

to give them attention. You can recognize these items in your backpack and carry it more securely.

2. *Present:* Learning to stay in your present moment is a muscle that needs exercising. Being present emotionally is not easy. It requires active self-dialogue guiding your choices. At first, this is challenging to retrain. Later, when automated, it becomes wisdom. Make a list of all the things you do without thinking, practicing those moments in full presence. You can become skilled at noticing when you are "going away." Tell your loved ones that you want to notice when your emotional presence light switch goes off. They will notice when you "go dark" in conversations. Set some rules for catching these moments so you can turn the light back on. You can picture the image of a light switch in your mind to help you turn on the light of presence again. It works!

3. *Potential:* Your potential is about your legacy and future, consciously directing your mind to regulate back to your best self. Our growth potential is the part of self that gives us great peace. I am familiar with my potential self. *She* is filled with the fruits of the spirit, granted by grace, and aligned with my values (Galatians 5:22–23). *She* makes choices from the virtues of love, joy, peace, patience, kindness, goodness, faithfulness, gentleness, and self-control. What does your potential self look like? Describe *who* you are striving to be. Let's be clear. It's not about what you have accomplished. Write an affirmation expressing your best-self intention—one that you read every day. It will keep you focused on your intent.

4. *Purpose*: What is the purpose of your life? What is the impact you strive to make? Mine is about my Christian walk. It guides everything I do. It is the legacy that guides my purpose. How do you want to be remembered after you are gone? By defining your big-picture purpose, it becomes your guide. At Delta, we talk about saving lives as our company mission. It guides *everything* we do. What is yours? Make sure you know it.

LESSON 6
Lean In!

Sheryl Sandberg's book *Lean In* sits on the bookshelf in my office. This phrase changed my life, directing me to address issues honestly and directly when necessary. In my clinical work, it has helped many people struggling with relationship problems, work issues, mental illness symptoms, and personal insecurity. "Lean into it" became my action phrase to face fear and teach others to override insecurity. When anxious, lean into it. When uncertain, lean into it. When overwhelmed, lean in. When avoiding, remember to lean in. Growth happens when we push ourselves to grow through uncomfortable moments. Practice the uncomfortable often, doing a little better each day.

This concept is counterintuitive at times. Let's get real. Leaning in freaks us out. It gives us stomachaches, headaches, tense faces, fearful looping thoughts, and excuses as to why we *can't* lean in. When we decide to be brave, we accept a difficult situation and rise to the challenge, accepting the feelings that go along with it as part of the process. It forces us to create new solutions that move us through that particular challenge. When I hear these words repeated back to me by my clients, I smile. Lean into your problems with strength from your past, applying new tools to reach your potential and purpose.

Here is an exercise for you. Identify which feelings and situations make you the most uncomfortable so that you lean into these experiences on purpose. Make a list of what you have control over in triggered situations, being clear about what you don't. Don't resist the uncomfortable feelings connected to the situation. Accept the strong emotion that comes with working through it. Blocking emotion keeps pain close. Not letting it go keeps it in your backpack too. The goal is to accept it and let it pass. Slowly enter difficult experiences, sitting in the discomfort for a few moments until it passes organically. When you allow discomfort for the purpose of growth, it loses its grip on you.

Think about the most challenging person you communicate with on a regular basis. Your mind will likely create a story that justifies not being around this person. It might tell you "you don't have time" or that person is "too difficult to be around" so that you stay out of emotional pain. When you lean in, you reject an unhelpful narrative and take a risk of discomfort for the purpose of creating a new story.

Pain need not control you unless you allow it. Emotional pain can be a great motivator and teacher. When you accept difficult emotions in order to manage the moment well, learning takes place. Be calm, clear, and consistent with how you are leading yourself through your pain points. Look for opportunities to practice the "lean in" and do this often to build your confidence in solving problems. You don't know what you are capable of until you work through the struggle. If you don't, you are missing out on something great.

When Tim asked me to come and work at Delta, I thought he was playfully paying me a compliment. I chuckled to myself but did not take it seriously until we spoke later about his vision. Honestly, I was unfamiliar with his company. The business world never interested me. I wanted to make an impact on people's lives. It wasn't long into my clinical practice when I started to see how clinical tools might benefit employees and corporate teams. Mental health is the same no matter where you are. It is a part of every person. As Tim and I talked over this opportunity, the light bulb went off in my mind. What I know needs to reach more people. These tools can be used in macro systems, not just in a treatment setting.

The more I leaned into the idea of therapy in the workplace, the more questions I had. Even though I was cautious, my internal voice was screaming, "Abso-fricken-lutely!" Despite strong internal fears of what could go wrong, I was excited that this option was even possible. I had the thought, so many times, that people should have therapy as a regular part of life without the insurance hassles, mental health clinic stigma, and the high cost financially. But could I translate this to the workplace? Would people step into my office, be vulnerable with true problems, and let me help them? What if it failed? Would leaving a strong clinical practice be wise?

Tim's innovative vision created an uncomfortable opportunity that I just had to lean into. This process was not easy for me. I had defined myself in a world governed by state confidentiality laws and the so-called prestige of being in a safe clinical world. I was at the top of my professional game and certain that I was carrying a big risk to fail in this endeavor. Nevertheless, I leaned in. I repeatedly asked basic questions about how to use the technology of business America and eventually figured out that I was standing in my own way to making this vision work. I needed to rely on the smart and savvy people around me, instead of thinking I had to do everything myself. It's a weakness to think you have to do things alone. Asking for help and leaning on others is wisdom. Learning to rely on others was a backpack moment that I needed to overcome.

I have observed cutting-edge execution at Delta. Although we are no stranger to problems, our navigation back to alignment with our core values is what leads us. The same is true for you. When you focus entirely on outcomes, you end up losing intention. When you focus on values you can accept failures as learning and lean in quickly to execute another attempt at getting it right. This repetitive process is how we learn regulation. The pattern of practice and failure leads to skill mastery. You can do that with just about anything.

Dive into unfamiliar challenges. Execute even when you are fearful. When you persist, you will eventually get it right. This requires intentional acceptance of when you screw it up, a key component of emotional security. Life is not about money or status. It's not about winning. Instead, it is about serving others in big-picture understanding. It is *we* over *me*, working through challenges together, and eventually getting it right.

Examine for a moment the lengths you have gone through in order to avoid having a difficult conversation. I am not judging, because I have done this too. It is easier to keep things status quo than to figure out how you will have that tough conversation. I am guilty of this in my professional life. For example, I will have a question that is worthy of asking but will tell myself, "Well, (that person) is too busy, and I shouldn't bother (him/her) with this information. It is probably something I should already know. I don't want to look stupid." Think about how this intellectualization makes me appear considerate rather than honest. If I am truthful, it is because I don't want to feel or appear stupid. When my *stupid* button goes off, I retreat rather than take initiative. This is about me, no one else. After the habit is established, my mindset becomes "well, this is just me." When you learn to lean into problems, you abandon old messages that distort your unhelpful view.

"Lean into it" is easier said than done. Addressing difficult emotions gives us all big hairy anxiety when we have to do anything that could potentially create a negative result. We crave certainty, not the unknown. The possibility of rejection, being wrong, or not being heard scares us. Take the risk to lean in so you are doing what is healthy and right, not what is easy. It's emotionally safe to walk away, feeling disappointed from a negative conversation. Walking away leads to ruminating on it or trying to block it. Soon you are judging, justifying, or feeling disconnected.

Leaning in to understand is accomplished by asking questions to better understand someone's response in a nonjudgmental energy. Relationship wins happen when you understand the other person, not when you agree or win the discussion. When you address problems from your most secure mindset, you develop control over your emotional energy, keeping words and tone helpful. Do you believe you can speak your perspective without negativity? Choose to let go of the outcome. Peace of mind results from executing the conversation skillfully, regardless of outcome. Leaning in is a healthy phrase to zip into your backpack. Put it where you can reach it, so you practice it often.

Here are some questions you can pull out of your backpack when difficult conversations arise:

1. I am not understanding; will you help me see things from your perspective?
2. What is your goal in this situation so I can see the big picture?
3. How am I negatively affecting you right now?
4. What can I do differently to resolve this with you peacefully?
5. Can we exchange feedback so we can work together on this issue?

Life lessons challenge us and bring consequences. I have lost friendships, family relationships, opportunities, and moments of happiness when I did not lean in quickly enough. Those moments were blind spots in my backpack. Yet, I press on, using what I know now, sharing it with you. Can you identify your unhelpful choices where you missed your opportunity to heal a negative situation? Have you avoided uncomfortable relationships or let fear prevent healing? Take a pause to reflect on the difficult moments of your past that developed your strengths. When you are able to identify what these moments taught you, then you can remove them from your backpack, making it lighter. Trust that you can do the work that it takes to move through those experiences in your backpack, developing the skills to lean into problems with full intention.

Lean into emotion.

Lean into an intentional mindset.

Lean into the best choice that gives you internal harmony and peace.

Intention + Practice = Mastery.

Lather, rinse, repeat.

Lean in, darn it! Just do it.

LESSON 7
Opposite Action Balance

The fascinating world of opposites has been a part of my clinical practice for many years. Opposite action balance is a principle of dialectical behavior therapy (DBT) that I encourage with many clients. This clinical framework focuses on four skill development areas: distress tolerance, emotion regulation, mindfulness, and interpersonal effectiveness. It assesses emotional skill level, providing tools to manage chronic patterns that interfere with both esteem and relationships.

In any struggle, when we find ourselves on one end of the spectrum, our power for creating balance lies in the opposite side. The pairing of opposites working together skillfully is useful for emotional balance. Can you be angry and have a peaceful presence? Are you capable of feeling sad but still find joy elsewhere? Can you notice your insecurity and take on a secure mindset at the same time? Polarities can work together, rather than compete. If used cooperatively, you direct yourself out of binary thinking.

For example, if you feel depressed and nurture the opposite action (joy), it creates balance. Your instinct in this emotion is to stay in low energy, remaining stuck in a sad emotion. You might find yourself listening to sad music, sleeping more, and numbing out on digital devices. These escape behaviors reinforce the problem. However, if you find something that creates joy and immerse your energy in that experience for the intention of balance, you lead yourself out of the depressed moment. Take, for example, anger or frustration. Your instinct may be to lash out, pull away, or to stew on the issue. If you observe your anger neutrally, feeding the opposite action (peacefulness), you will get a better outcome. By nurturing the opposite in mood, mindset, and behavior, you regulate quickly.

I have witnessed clients chronically stuck in negativity patterns learn how to find balance by using this method. When stuck in intense emotion, our habits are consumed by hurt. Emotional paralysis or perfectionism can develop from these deep hurts. Extremes drive imbalance, leading to all-or-nothing patterns. Automatic pilot habits enter the picture and intention goes out the window. Our brains seek activities to feel better, wanting habits of pleasure or comfort.

When I learned about opposite correction from Marsha Linehan, a CBT therapist and author, I found myself teaching and practicing it. For example, take periods of strong fatigue. This could be feeling tired, stressed out, or frustrated. What happens when you repeatedly notice your emotion? Your repetitive self-observation develops an emotional pattern of circular thinking. By observing the pattern of noticing the stuck feeling, you can spot your habit. Shifting your body, mind, and behavior to the opposite, you can learn to regulate energy and intention that leads you out of the habit. This was exciting for me to learn and teach. This tool repairs energy patterns that can keep people fluctuating between their highs and lows.

In situations of high fear, you can focus on the courage to work through the fear. In moments of apathy, you can practice engagement in the problem. When bored, you can become curious, learning a new skill that replaces boredom with excitement. In self-doubt, you can practice confident courage, letting the insecurity pass. When suffering, you can focus on choices that support healing, rather than believing your pain story. When you think you know better than someone else, but decide to ask questions to learn instead, you build connection and insight. This method of opposite action creates an easy map to follow.

- When in fear, practice courage.
- When in anger, practice peace.
- When in apathy, practice engagement.
- When in boredom, practice curiosity.
- When in envy, practice contentment.
- When lonely, practice connection.
- When in worry, practice letting go.
- When in doubt, practice confidence.
- When in pain, focus on the practice of healing.

There are many other opposite pairings to identify. If you tend to block emotion, you can learn to identify and lean into the emotion so you can talk skillfully about it. If you attach to emotion, you can learn to notice this and direct yourself away from the loop.

Whether noticing sadness, irritation, or feeling overwhelmed, you can lead yourself out through an opposite action. What extremes do you spot in your habits? Identify your opposite partners for authentic skill practice. Remaining in unproductive habits is like circling a roundabout traffic crossing without ever exiting. By exiting you get to your destination. Your exit is leaning into the opposite action solution. What you pay attention to in conflict moments becomes your destination. What you decide to practice is the exit to your roundabout. This backpack lesson stops the looping patterns of your mind. Watch out for thinking roundabouts and exit quickly.

LESSON 8
Video Game Communication

People fascinate me with their unique traits and contributions. Most want to do the right thing but get caught up in moments of internal or external conflict. Intending to do harm is not common. However, skill deficiency *is* common. Being skilled in communication requires practicing new ways of showing up for our loved ones.

Video game communication is about leading conversations to deeper levels in order to understand needs fully, not staying on level one or two, where the game is easy to play. When playing video games, the fun of playing is advancing to the higher levels where the challenges and rewards are more thrilling. If you only played as far as level one, you would miss out on so many facets of the game. The same is true for people.

When I was in clinical practice, I had a colleague who would teach clients the definition of intimacy (another word for connection). She went on to say that intimacy means into-me-see. She would remind clients that they are responsible for teaching others how to see things through their eyes, encouraging this respect in both directions. Genuine curiosity requires interest in the thoughts and feelings of others. It demands self-control, with a focus on active listening rather than responding. Curiosity comes from an open mindset, nurturing connection through understanding differences.

Advanced communication requires us to ask many questions when we sense our words are negatively impacting others. Doing the work to understand someone else's perspective may be uncomfortable, but this is what next-level connection requires. Empathy is an essential emotional skill that helps you do just that. Like any skill, empathy needs to be understood and regulated. When we are quick to take offense, empathy is no longer leading. When we react defensively, empathy subsides. Asking questions to seek clarity builds trust through empathic communication.

Here are some helpful empathic responses that encourage deeper communication:

- Help me understand your thoughts on this issue a little better.
- Can you give me an example so I can apply this idea?
- How does my behavior affect you emotionally when we disagree?

The "I know this already" perspective that arises in conflict shuts down curiosity. Asking questions does not mean you agree or that you have the wrong perspective. It is simply asking questions to get a deeper-level understanding of perspective. It is a thorough process of making sure you clearly understand the other person (because you care) before presenting your view. Curiosity is a key to wisdom. When you train your brain to replace defensiveness with curiosity, you lead the resolve process quicker or more effectively.

At Delta, we practice listening to understand rather than listening to respond. This practice is written on our walls and actively encouraged. It is not easy, because we are wired to know the answer for purposes of seeking validation. From a young age, we are reinforced to have the right answer. This confidence-building process is how the education system is set up. If you don't listen in school, you won't know the answers. When people have the right answer, they are validated for knowing and this feels good. It is essential to learning. Developing your voice is equally important. How else can you stand up for what you believe? It is how learning is reinforced.

Delta's organizational culture lives and breathes the principles from the Arbinger Institute, an organization that provides resources for top leadership to drive optimal results through examining mindset. I love their books because they shifted me from theory to self-application. One of the concepts that they taught me was about seeing the experience of others and adjusting my efforts based on this awareness. We like to hear about how our positive behavior affects others. Validation makes us feel good. But can we be secure enough to hear about how our negative behavior affects others? Can we admit our flaws without this leading to emotional injury? If we can, curiosity will be your self-development skill.

Here is the challenge. Find someone you trust. Ask them, "When I am in a negative headspace, how does my negative behavior affect you?" *My friend, deep inside you know that it does.* As a result of our flaws, we all create negative moments. How do your negative moments impact your "inner circle" relationships? If you think you are above knowing this information, you will not find your way to the deeper feelings of those around you. You are strong enough to hear the answers. Be brave and be curious for the sake of deeper connection.

When the conversation gets difficult, remember to keep going. Ask questions about your questions so that you fully understand. Get to the advanced level where deep connection awaits you!

LESSON 9
People, Trains, and Villages

Examine your relationship with yourself for a moment. Your self-view is assessed by how you talk to yourself in your mind. We don't really learn how to do this. The difficult seasons of life often lead us into examination. Thoughts just happen, resulting from habit. Most are connected to memory, involving emotional triggers and patterns that have been there consistently over time. When a negative thought pops up, it tends to be prompted by either an internal or external experience. Unless you are mindfully present, you may not even notice it. Your ability to direct your thinking comes from thought awareness, skillful self-talk, and keeping a mindset based on helpful paradigms in your belief system.

Negative thoughts naturally occur when challenges arise. You can spot negativity when emotional tanks are low or in competitive situations. Also, when you are frustrated in the mastery of a new experience, it shows up. When I think of the power of mindset, I visualize three things that provide perspective: *people*, *trains*, and *villages*.

I like to visualize our thoughts as people roaming about a train station. There are all sorts of individuals (thoughts) at this station. Some are optimistic, negative, ambivalent, emotional, pragmatic, productive, etc. As a mentally healthy individual, you get to choose which train to board, each train providing transportation to the village to which you want to go. If you consider the train you board as the internal dialogue that you choose in response to your thoughts, you either hop on a train that is helpful or one that is not. The different trains take you to a mindset village that will either be helpful or not.

Your self-talk—the train you board—can be one that frames any given situation in a secure, peaceful, or productive way. When you board one that is based in negative emotion, it impacts your internal experience, leading to misery. When you take the wrong train, you end up in a story of blame. Blame stories ignite the situation further, leading to more negative emotion. How you perceive the situation and dialogue through the challenging moment either brings peace or fuels the conflict. When you take the mentally healthy train, your self-talk is accountable and observational rather than reactionary. It is an opportunity to see the good in others, focusing on solutions rather than problems. This train of thinking brings problem-solving that allows your experience to be meaningful.

Your mindset—the way in which you choose to look at any given situation—is the village in which you end up residing. This village contains beliefs that allow you to see yourself and others in the best possible light, regardless of the challenge. This does not mean taking on a Pollyanna view where you are happy and positive all the time. It is not about putting on a happy face or avoiding the problem. It is a way to gift yourself the most productive story to view a situation from a secure mindset. Fear creates an unhealthy story, blocking intention. By nurturing helpful thoughts, you can reprogram your mind to seek connection through curiosity for understanding and mutual solutions. When you learn to ask more questions in moments of frustration (rather than just give opinions), you collaborate and grow at the same time. Being healthy is about learning, not about being right or being in charge.

Take time to observe your thoughts. Decide clearly to get on the productive-internal-dialogue train that takes you to a helpful mind-set village. If you are on the wrong train, you will feel it in your connection with others and your sense of emotional security. The good news is when you notice you are on the wrong train, you can get off at the next stop (backpack securely in place) and board the right one. If you do that over and over, you will eventually board this train in habit, arriving easily at your destination.

LESSON 10
Lead with Gratitude. It Creates Meaningful Connection.

It's easy to be inconsistent with gratitude. As creatures of habit, we frequently operate on automatic pilot, rather than living with intention. Retraining requires constant practice. I believe it is the reason why we *think* about our goals but are inconsistent or slow to *accomplish* them. Thinking is awareness. Doing is regulation. Saying what you are grateful for gives joy to both giver and receiver. When in your authentic self, you create moments of connection with gratitude. Too much time is spent on worrying how to speak feelings (both positive and negative) in fear of how it will be received. Speaking your truth, in love, is wisdom. It gives energy to your purpose. Sharing gratitude can be your best habit. Work on being present with those around you so that you show up for them when they need it. Speak gratitude often, don't just think it.

As a Christian, I practice gratitude because of what God has done for me through Jesus, my Savior. I am called for this practice. Healing from hurt is essential. Unresolved hurt blocks gratitude, leading to more hurt. Gratitude for the gifts that pain brings to our lives promotes healing. It can live in your backpack and travel with you everywhere you go.

I remember the day that my sweet grandmother passed away. My father's mother was the opposite of my angry maternal grandmother. Grama Annie was a unique, happy energy in my life. She was proud of everything I did. She modeled contentment. Simple and kind, she looked me in the face when she spoke with me. She showed up for me, which is such a beautiful experience. Her infectious giggle was so big that it made me laugh too. When she passed away, I was with her, holding her hand. I treasure that moment in my heart forever.

I was a mother of three young children when she died. I remember getting the call that she was in the hospital on life support. It was December, just weeks before Christmas. I was taking my graduate school finals. I arrived at the hospital where my family was sitting in the lounge visiting. Grama was alone in her room, hooked up to machines. I couldn't understand why no one was with her, holding her hand to comfort her. My sister and I went to the room and we sat with her. I remember being at her side for days, until she passed. Despite my great sadness for what was coming, I held her hand, recounting memories of love between us. As I retold these stories, she squeezed my hand over and over. I was in serenity knowing that I was present in one of the most important moments of her life, just as she had been there for me so many times when I needed it. When she took her last breath, I felt an unexplainable peace that made me know that there is a God who calls us home and that our journey truly matters.

Grama Annie died on the same day that her husband passed away seventeen years earlier. She loved and relied on him in her marriage. Their playful modeling led me to seek that in my own relationship. Grama had little money. She had no career—not even a driver's license. But what she did have, I wanted. She was filled with gratitude for the challenging life she had been given without complaint. She accepted her life for exactly what it was. I wish I would have shared my gratitude with her more often. Something deep inside tells me that she already knew.

Gratitude is underrated. When stuck in depression, grief, or anxiety, practice gratitude. Accept your failures and work on getting back on track using gratitude as your guide. Watch out for "what if, should, why and oh no!" moments that drain gratitude and keep you in the hurt. Stop telling yourself messages about how hard life is. Instead, take each day as it comes, leading from blessings, not from pain.

As I age, I see the tapestry God has sewn in my life and in those around me. I know that I will never be perfect at seeing His grand picture. The hurts keep me humble, close, and strong. I have many faults. I get stuck in my hurt habits just like you. However, I will never give up at figuring it out, leaning into moments that God has before me, for the purpose of loving others like the overwhelming love He has shown to me.

Gratitude leads connection.

Gratitude nurtures forgiveness.

Gratitude heals.

Gratitude helps us let go of what does not belong to us.

Set a goal to practice gratitude at least three times a day for thirty days. Replace complaining with gratitude. Notice when you drain your energy with negativity. This awareness belongs to you. You can't prevent thoughts, but you can navigate through them. How you choose to reset when you are exhausted is your backpack responsibility. Carry it skillfully, my friend. Carry it with a lens that practices gratitude.

This communication practice works well with others too. When you address problems with others, begin and end your conversations with gratitude. It makes such a difference.

KEEPING YOUR BACKPACK LIGHT

"Faith allows us to confidently walk with God into a future filled with joy; one that can become an extraordinary and amazing adventure."

—MARY C. NEAL

In order to keep your backpack light, you must notice what weighs you down and practice letting it go. This means making sure the size of your backpack doesn't have capacity for everyone else's stuff, only yours. How you see each item in your backpack determines the weight of your load. How strong you see yourself also affects how you carry it and what you focus on along the way.

I apply this when I choose to see the beauty of the hike around me, not focusing on how heavy my backpack is, in any given difficulty. Now this practice isn't pretending that the load is light. When we have good awareness, we know the weight of our stress. It is consciously choosing to focus on the beauty, despite the burden. I think this is where we go wrong. We get stuck circling or avoiding problems. How we see problems matters. How heavy do you make the frustrations that arise in your daily experience?

Your internal dialogue will either free or contaminate your mind.

- "Boy, is this heavy. I don't think I can do this anymore. This is breaking me. Why is this happening to me? What if___ happens? I will never be the same!"
- "Boy, this is heavy. I know I can handle it. I will carry this knowing that it is making me stronger. I will manage it to the best of my ability."

Next, define how you will carry it with the right mindset. Write out a helpful phrase that will keep you on track. Decide who you want to walk next to you during the struggle. Know which tools you will keep close to you. If you do these things, the struggle will not consume you and you will keep walking forward.

Take a moment to step back to see the problem as a later gain so you don't give energy to the triggered experience, but instead the big-picture view.

Here are three things you can journal to keep your backpack light:

1. What thoughts are weighing you down when you face difficulty? Examine your past, present, and future fears. Make a list so you can spot them and remind yourself to let them go. As you journal, the goal is to acknowledge your fears and work through them. Although this is difficult, it is necessary for you to establish a contract with yourself to stop giving energy to your pain points. When hurt arises again in the future, honor your contract by reminding yourself that you already chose to let it go. Doing this as often as you need is a healing practice.
2. Identify habits aligned with your values that keep you moving forward. This reflection nurtures your wellness voice. Which habits are not aligned with them? How will you begin changing these habits?
3. Make a list of the life lessons that you will keep in your backpack to help you be resilient under stress. Include: people who have taught you (literary or real experience), mantras that sustain you in difficult times, and the tools that you use when you need them.

By reflecting on these truths, you keep your backpack light for whatever life brings. Navigate back to your strong, best version of self when the hike gets difficult. Do that every time.

FOR YOUR BACKPACK

Do not pick up or carry anyone's backpack but your own. The emotional security of how you carry your backpack defines the boundaries that influence your relationship with self and others.

THE BACKPACKS
OF OTHERS

———

"Your beliefs become your thoughts,
Your thoughts become your words,
Your words become your actions,
Your actions become your habits,
Your habits become your values,
Your values become your destiny."

—MAHATMA GANDHI

RESPECTING BOUNDARIES

Boundaries are reasonable and safe guidelines we establish in order to live in a healthy way. They allow time and space for intentional habits, define priorities, and help with managing relationships. Ultimately, they become the dos and don'ts of our lifestyle choices based on our specific needs. If healthy, our limits encourage equity in relationships as well as when to be assertive in moments when situations feel unfair. When we are uncomfortable, they guide us to stand up for what we want, so that we keep our choices aligned with our values. Unhealthy boundaries lead to internal conflict, which often fuels emotion, escalating insecurities and creating unreasonable expectations in relationships. When boundaries are rigid, they create emotional distance with those we love. If they are loose, they lead to power struggles and feelings of being taken advantage of in a relationship.

Rigid boundaries can be like locking your home and never letting anyone in or out. Loose boundaries are like leaving your door unlocked all the time, letting anyone (including strangers) go in and out and do as they wish. Clearly defined boundaries help us know what is acceptable based on personal values and self-respect. Respecting the boundaries of others, based on their backpack experience, is crucial to healthy interaction.

In order to be healthy, people need boundaries in many areas of life including:

- Priorities with time
- Relationships
- Physical space/touch
- Communication
- Electronic devices
- Responsibilities
- Self-care habits

Poor boundaries fuel insecurities about how you are perceived, resulting in people-pleasing behavior. Allowing fear or guilt to lead your choices will end in anxiety. Healthy boundaries are about being true to your needs. Although it isn't easy, you can learn to let go of the fear of disappointing others. Recognize when you attach to how others perceive you, so you can shift gears. Instead, direct your attention to your best choice, letting go of the emotion that drives your need for acceptance.

When you focus on peaceful alignment with your values, you can be secure, even if others are unhappy with you in the moment. After repeated practice of operating from your secure inner voice, you will have less anxiety about what others think and do. With confidence, you can communicate your needs clearly, celebrating differences, without taking it personally.

When it comes to the backpacks of others, your loved ones get to define their needs, even if you don't like what those limits entail.

Ask yourself:

- Are there people in my life that I try to control or change?
- Do I push back when others set limits or say "no" to my requests?
- Does the behavior of others affect my happiness, particularly when they don't do what I want?
- What specific boundaries do I need to respect in my relationships?

Jarrod, a client in his fifties, struggled with accepting the boundaries of his wife and children, leading to high-conflict patterns. Raised in a strict patriarchal home, he was rigid about their lifestyle (meals, priorities, religion, politics, and who his family members could spend time with when not with him). His wife complained that he was unreasonable, jealous, and demanded attention often. His therapy focused on accepting the needs of his wife and children, not expecting them to have the same as his own. By using the backpack boundaries, Jarrod was able to hear about the needs of his family members, understanding how his rigid requests were emotionally affecting his wife and children. Over time he was able to loosen unhelpful rules, making boundaries adjustments, and communicating with his wife and children respectfully.

Boundaries connect us to our values. When inconsistent, relationships can be confusing. Allowing others to make their decisions, based on what they are comfortable with, keeps you out of their backpack. Remember, you can learn to respect differences. What others need to do to manage their lives is up to them. Accepting this principle allows you to let go of false control to change what you do not like about them.

What controlling behaviors do you need to let go of in your relationships? This might be letting go of your partner's dietary preferences or how they choose to spend their downtime. Maybe you need to let go of fashion preferences with your adolescent child. Or maybe it's judgment against a friend with opposing political views. Stay out of their backpack. Your backpack will be easier to carry if you let others live by their boundaries, just as you live by yours.

When you love people, it is natural to want them to have healthy habits to manage their life well. You may find yourself in your loved one's backpack easily. Notice this quickly so you can take your hands out of it.

When I shared this philosophy with my family, the phrase "not your backpack" became a part of our family culture. Now when I am trying to push my agenda, I am reminded of this by a family member. When I hear the phrase, I stop preaching my perspective and pivot quickly in a new direction. You can do the same. Keeping our hands out of the backpack of others is not always easy, but it is healthy. Keep practicing!

AUTHENTIC, KIND HONESTY

"Let gratitude be the pillow upon which you kneel to say your nightly prayer. And let faith be the bridge you build to overcome evil and welcome good."

—MAYA ANGELOU

One of the kindest things we can do is being honest with others. This is not brutal honesty, because being brutal is not about honesty, it is about control. It's not partial honesty to protect feelings and prevent conflict. Partial honesty is not honesty either because it is rooted in fear. Kind honesty is sharing your real feelings in warm, emotional energy using clear *I-statements* without overtalking or avoiding a difficult interaction. Bottling up feelings is as toxic as ruminating on them. Consistency with healthy honesty requires practice. It looks like this:

I feel _____ when _____.
I need _____.

Kindness is speaking the truth in love, sharing feelings without an agenda. Kind honesty is about exchanging perspective without needing agreement or full understanding of your view. You are responsible for you, not them.

When others do things that you do not like, notice your reactive feelings without attaching to them or creating a negative story in your mind. Your ability to pause—sitting momentarily in your feelings—will help you respond in a way that includes kindness. When you learn to do this regularly, the negative responses of others will bother you less and less. When blame is no longer your story, it is easier to be kind in how you manage any difficult situation.

Notice the moments when you lack warmth in how you interact

with others. Rather than making an excuse about why you are short-tempered, dig kindness out of the value section of your backpack and lean back in. Being kind and honest is doing your part. Making decisions based on your values is about honoring your contract with yourself. It is not about anyone else. Kindness is about who you are, regardless of circumstance. It is good manners. Simply put, it is the right thing to do.

SELF-RESPECT LEADS PEACEFUL CONNECTION

"One of the truest signs of maturity is the ability to disagree with some-one while still remaining respectful."

—DAVE WILLIS

In mental health, we often talk about one's relationship with self, which is connected to esteem. When you consistently operate from clear boundaries, esteem results. Self-respect nurtures respect in your relationships. This is observable in how you react to emotional situations. It is also evident in how you manage authority and self-discipline. How quickly you execute solutions in tough moments demonstrates your skill level. When you are secure, you can show restraint, sharing opinions at the right time and in a helpful way.

The concept of esteem has been misunderstood by many, especially in faith circles. I have heard the misinformed parrot these false views, which have led to negative views about religion as a whole.

HERE ARE A FEW SELF-ESTEEM MYTHS I HAVE HEARD:

Myth 1: *Self-esteem problems are a deficiency in faith living. Those with low esteem have weak faith.* This myth leads to self-righteous thinking, creating judgment that belongs to God. Discernment is about one's ability to accurately appraise a situation. Discernment is necessary; judgment is not. We are not better or worse than anyone else. We can see only a glimpse of a person's struggles. Taking a superiority perspective when someone is hurting leads to spiritual confusion. Esteem is not a character flaw.

Myth 2: *Self-esteem is selfish and consuming.* Not true. It is a part of sinful human nature to have moments of selfishness and to be consumed by insecurity. Self-esteem is a part of the emotional growth process that often leads to change. It is not black and white. Nor is it exclusive to those who have identified an internal battle in their feelings about self. One's experience, habits, child-rearing, negative memories, and willingness to develop insight impact this growth. When someone goes through hardship, it is an opportunity to grow out of the discomfort that they feel and usually leads to perspective, awareness, and insight.

Myth 3: *Something bad has to happen in your life in order for you to struggle with self-esteem.* False. Distorted thinking about self comes from internal and external repetition. It is often a habit or thought pattern that is not discussed or addressed until it is revealed by the person in distress.

Myth 4: *People cannot change their self-esteem. It's a part of one's personality.* Also not true. Whatever we focus on in our thinking and choices can be changed over time with awareness and practiced intention.

Myth 5: *Self-esteem problems are a sign of personal weakness and should be kept secret.* The truth is that being vulnerable and transparent with those who have earned the honor to hear your feelings can help you change negative esteem patterns. When people stop covering up how they feel, growth toward a secure mindset develops. Those who sit in judgment have the choice to remain in their ignorance or fear.

Myth 6: *Some people don't struggle at all with esteem.* Anyone who has tapped into the deeper realm of their existence will observe the internal battle of their mind. Blocking an unpleasant emotion results in poor awareness of feelings, leading to disconnection in relationships. Likewise, obsessively being concerned with what others think of you fuels insecurity. Struggling with esteem is a battle that often develops awareness. It's a process, not an outcome. It's a starting block to growth if the person struggling is brave enough to lean into it.

Myth 7: *People who have self-esteem lack humility.* You can be humble and appreciate who you are at the same time. Remember that arrogance is insecurity and shame in disguise. A secure person can have esteem and faith at the same time, knowing what belongs to God and what belongs to them is part of free will. In *The Purpose Driven Life: What on Earth Am I Here For?*, Rick Warren wrote, "True humility is not thinking less of yourself; it is thinking of yourself less." We have to be careful of dichotomous thinking that is riddled with assumptions and judgments. When we believe we fully understand others, we fall into superiority thinking, which creates bias. What others do is not our concern. What we do belongs to us.

Self-esteem requires self-acceptance of your strengths and weaknesses. Awareness of needed growth leads to behaviors that sustain healthy living. Setting clear expectations with others helps you to live in accordance with the standards you set for yourself.

Self-esteem is directly tied to the respect you give others. Those lacking esteem are often at risk for placing a partner's needs over their own or needing to control the relationship. Self-respect leads to partnership, collaboration, and cooperation. When your self-respect is poor, so is your response to others.

When you are emotionally secure, true respect looks like this:

- Gentleness in thoughts and words
- Patience over irritation
- Peaceful startup to difficult conversations
- Accountability over blame
- Equality mindset, not keeping score
- Seeking clarity and solutions following questions to fully understand
- Accepting of flaws and able to identify strengths
- Inviting accountability challenges for growth
- Refusing to take the choices of others personally
- Willingness to see the other person's perspective, even in conflict
- Open, honest, and transparent conversation, not emotionally distant or needy

TRUST IS EARNED

"Trust is like blood pressure. It's silent, vital to good health, and if abused it can be deadly."

—FRANK SONNENBERG

Trust is a crucial part of any relationship, regardless of the connection. When it is broken, it is hard to rebuild. Repeated fractures in trust can lead to estranged relationships that were once functional and enjoyable. Different from respect, trust is earned through consistent healthy choices over an extended time period. We can forgive without trust. Forgiveness is about you, releasing the negativity that comes from holding onto hurt. Trust is about the other person consistently earning that honor.

How do you know if someone deserves your trust? In truth, you don't. Individuals have different tolerances for broken trust. If someone is not able to see how they are hurting you repeatedly, making excuses for their behavior without owning their part, trust may not be repaired. Sincere accountability helps you know when someone is worthy of more chances for closeness, learning from errors that have caused others hurt. Maya Angelou said it perfectly, "When someone shows you who they are, believe them the first time."

When trust is damaged by repeated betrayals, it is healthy to have strict boundaries that protect you from enabling an unhealthy pattern of inequality. If relationship rules are not reciprocal, it can lead to one person working harder in the relationship, which will eventually lead to resentment and more conflict. If real effort to change the trust dynamic continues, the relationship may be salvaged. However, if a pattern of betrayal is not changed, remaining in the unhealthy dynamic might be more damaging. Knowing your deal-breaker limits and bottom-line expectations are important to making this decision. The consistent accountability of the betrayer shows willingness for change.

My client Sandra discovered that her husband was interacting online with other women. Periodically when he felt neglected, he would secretly engage in what he called "harmless banter" with other women. When limits were discussed, he began lying, minimizing his emotional betrayals, until she again discovered his indiscretions. One of the women randomly reached out to Sandra inquiring whether they were divorced. After meeting together several times to address this pattern, Sandra's husband stopped attending. Lacking accountability, his betrayal habits continued, forcing Sandra to initiate divorce. Regardless of efforts to make him happy, she couldn't change him. She could only focus on her backpack, accepting the sadness that went with his refusal to align with the values she held dear. When it comes to the backpack of others, we can't fix or make others change. Our best choice lies in focusing on our own.

In situations involving differences in personal preferences, the general rule is to stay out of the backpacks of others. However, if the situation involves major value violations (trust betrayals), it is up to you to set things straight by being clear and consistent about what you need.

Here are some examples of healthy trust boundaries:

- Your time limits for helping are respected. Always be clear about how much time you can give.
- Crisis is infrequent, rather than patterned. If frequent, refer to professional counseling.
- When you help, it is appreciated with warmth, not demanded or expected.
- You are not responsible for duties that the requestor is capable of doing independently. *Doing for* is not the same as providing emotional support.

Be cautious if you are repeatedly creating solutions for others, which creates advice-giving dependency. Relationships must be reciprocal. Anytime you are responsible for doing more than your part, the relationship will lack balance.

If you find yourself in relationships where others depend on you to feel better or keep them going, verbalize fair boundaries. If this is not respected or accepted, then take a big step back. You are not helping. The goal is to be connected, without thinking or doing for those who need to figure their lessons out. Esteem comes from figuring things out yourself. Don't steal that gift from others.

Your boundaries around trust do not come from your feelings but from your loved one's consistent behavior. Trust allows you to keep alignment with your values, which is why you have such a strong reaction to those who violate your values. If you don't have clear limits defined in your relationships, it is time that you do. Forgiveness helps you to be healthy inside. Trust is warranted when it is consistently earned through accountability. Be clear about what you need to build trust with those in your life. Honoring your values builds confidence. Dishonoring them breeds self-doubt. If you don't know and understand your needs based on your values, you won't be able to communicate clearly.

Similarly, be trustworthy with others. Your word and actions matter. Do what you say and say what you do. If your reactions are unpredictable, you impact others negatively when they need your support. When you provide emotional safety through supportive messages, others are invited to openly share difficult feelings. If this is the case in your experience, you are doing something right. However, if others shy away from you, not sharing their feelings with you, then you have empathy work to do to communicate in a way that nurtures emotional safety and trust.

The experience of others is so complicated that we can't possibly understand their unique thoughts and feelings that lead to their choices. If you have been neglected in your life, the result can be a pattern of blocking emotions because you have not been taught how to speak about them eloquently. On the other side, if you have been rescued emotionally in your life, you are likely to struggle with unregulated emotion because of high emotional needs. Because our backpacks are so different, judgment needs to be eliminated. Accepting this as a rule to your relationships can keep you out of bias for the unique backpack that others in your life carry.

Do you find yourself getting hung up on why people do what they do? Does the negative behavior of others remain in your thoughts after you leave them? If so, choose to let that go, knowing that it does not belong to you. Accept those who have earned your trust, believe that they are doing the best they can, and show up when they ask for help. By noticing differences from a peaceful mindset, you allow others to carry their own backpack, figuring out what they need to learn as they walk the path of life. Based on this insight, where can you make changes in your relationships? Write down your first step toward positive change.

I say, do it now.

FOR YOUR BACKPACK

Clear emotional boundaries help you stay out of the backpacks of others. Be calm and clear about your boundaries, choosing kindness and self-respect when communicating in difficult situations. Alignment with your values helps you do just that!

GOD'S BACKPACK

"Consider a tree for a moment. As beautiful as trees are to look at, we don't see what goes on underground—as they grow roots. Trees must develop roots in order to grow strong and produce their beauty. But we don't see the roots. We just see and enjoy the beauty. In much the same way, what goes on inside of us is like the roots of a tree."

—JOYCE MEYER

LETTING GO COMPLETELY

Trusting God completely is a struggle for just about everyone. Our flawed human nature and the desire to control outcomes get in our way. We see things from our small lens, which is not the lens of God, who sees it all. What will it take for you to trust God with healing your past? Will you trust Him in guiding your present struggles? Can you decide to securely embrace your future with hope and purpose? When in worry, we circle around what we *should* do, rather than knowing with certainty that we are being nurtured for growth as we move through pain. This anxiety blocks our big-picture perspective.

I remember a phone call with my older sister in my early years of motherhood. I was worried about my eighteen-month-old daughter, who was hospitalized at the time. I remember being overwhelmed with fear and she said something profound to me. She asked me if I had given this worry to God and if I was truly trusting Him with that worry. "Of course I did!" I responded. I will never forget what she said. "Holly, if you laid this worry at the cross, why did you pick it back up again?" In that moment I understood what it meant to let go of what did not belong to me. Our daughter was in the hospital and I couldn't do anything about it. I was doing everything possible as her parent, but God had this one in His backpack. "Let go of what is not yours. God is in charge," she insisted. Although the outcome didn't belong to me, the process for managing it did. I focused on staying present and committed to what was in my control. I reminded myself that God created her and loved her as His dear child. His love was and will always be more powerful than mine. My daughter was on loan to me for an undetermined amount of time and I could serve Him in how I handled this scary situation.

My daughter bounced back quickly, and I was graced not to carry this burden long. Years later, when our two-week-old youngest child was hospitalized with a collapsed lung from a respiratory infection, I pulled out this defining backpack moment and it sustained me through the fear that once again rose to the surface. God loves all His children. My perspective is so narrow. Yours is too.

What are the worries that you hold in your heart, dear friend? Your worry might be connected to health, finances, or relationship. Can you let God guide the master plan, while you manage your part to the best of your ability? Emotions pass. Even intense, deep-rooted feelings pass with practice. You can decide to focus on the pain itself or on the journey of working through the pain, awaiting the strength on the other side of hurt.

Many people carry intense pain around with them. Your backpack may be large and the load heavy. It may feel so big that you can't imagine letting go and moving forward. I hold those who have hurts from loss and tragedy close to my heart. The road is not easy to move through suffering. Letting go does not mean that the pain is gone. It doesn't mean you forget. No, it means that when that pain resurfaces, you choose to honor it by sitting with it until it moves through you once again. This is navigating pain, not attaching to it or blocking it. It is the key to doing your part and letting God do the rest.

Being angry at God is pointless and self-serving. Blaming Him for anything connected to another person's unhealthy choice is simply a limited perspective. Pain helps us. We don't choose it, but neither does He. Our response to negative life events belongs to us. Learning to step outside your pain will provide healthy perspective. Decide to let go of poisonous anger. He does not choose to hurt you.

If you are a parent, ask yourself these questions: If something negative happens to your child while at school, is that your fault? If they get hurt outside, did you do that? Just as you do not make bad things happen to your children, neither does God. But like a parent, He can comfort you through your hurt, just as you do for your child. Sometimes those seasons seem to take forever. The difficult periods bring patience if you allow this to change you for the better. Let go. Let go. Let go. This too shall pass. Seek the wisdom He gives you. Stop focusing on the hurt.

When I worked in residential treatment, I developed a bond with a troubled young man. Neil was a fourteen-year-old gang member that found himself caught up in a world of drugs and violence. His conduct issues led to out-of-home placement. I recall our spiritual discussions and his resistance to religious conversations. After months of resistance, he asked me to explain religion in terms he could understand. I asked him for thirty days of intention to run a spiritual experiment.

I explained that a Christian's life is based on two main principles: *what God does* and *what we do* with the right mindset. Neil willingly gave me the freedom to write (using a Sharpie) on the back of his hands. On his left hand, I wrote "Thy Will Be Done." On his right hand, I wrote "All Glory to God." The truth on his left hand was God's job. When we know Him closely, God protects, guides, and directs our journey for our greater good. With perspective we do not have, He takes our difficult moments and turns them into learning that strengthens us. We can trust that He will lead us through anything, making us stronger and better through endurance.

I went on to say that the instruction written on his right hand belongs to us. Our journey is about doing our part, giving glory to God in *all* that we do, out of love for what He has done for us through His son, Jesus. I suggested that when Neil felt emotionally stuck, he could teach himself to pause and decide which hand would lead him. In that place of pause, he could ask himself: does this situation belong to God? If it does, let go and trust His plan. I went on to say that when we listen, He guides us through His Word and the faithful people He places along our path.

I told Neil, if the situation belonged to him (something he was responsible for), he needed to follow the boundaries led by the values God lovingly gave him in Scripture. His decisions were his choice, done in peace and out of love to glorify God, not himself. We practiced and discussed this awareness over and over in the weeks ahead. When the thirty days were up, he asked to continue the experiment. Months later he shared that he wanted these teachings tattooed on his body when he was older to remind him of this spiritual lesson. I wonder if he got them. After leaving our facility, I never saw him again. All I know is that this backpack moment was tattooed on my brain. Forever. Serving Neil reinforced my own boundaries when it came to what belonged to me and what belonged to God.

Understanding the spiritual journey is about walking with God, trusting Him with your hurts. It involves seeing His direction and feeling the beauty in all of His children as you move through the ups and downs of your experience. He gives us what we need. He says in II Corinthians 12:9, "My grace is sufficient for you." We can trust that all things will turn out for our good in the end, even when the items in our backpack are heavy and hurtful. Faith is about trusting the process. When we surrender hurts, accepting only our small part, the hurts strengthen us for new experiences.

In my backpack, I carry favorite Bible passages that remind me of how I choose to live, regardless of the circumstances. I share them with you. If you share my walk with Christ, have you identified which passages you want to keep in your backpack, so you can let Him carry what you don't have control over? Make your list of backpack passages that guide you through tough moments when you need them. Memorize them so they will be in your heart. Knowing what belongs to me and what belongs to Him helps me skillfully carry my backpack. It will help you carry yours too!

MY BACKPACK PASSAGES

Acceptance: Proverbs 19:21, "Many are the plans in a man's heart, but it is the Lord's purpose that prevails."

Anger: James 1:19–20, "Everyone should be quick to listen, slow to speak, and slow to become angry, for anger does not bring about the righteous life that God desires."

Attitude: Philippians 2:14, "Do everything without complaining or arguing."

Comfort: Psalm 46:1–2a, "God is our refuge and strength, an ever-present help in trouble. Therefore, I will not fear."

Commitment: Galatians 6:9, "Let us not become weary in doing good, for at the proper time we will reap a harvest if we do not give up."

Confidence: Philippians 4:13, "I can do everything through Him who gives me strength."

Courage: II Timothy 1:7, "For God did not give us a spirit of timidity, but a spirit of power, of love and of self-discipline."

Criticism: Matthew 7:1–2, "Do not judge, or you too will be judged. For in the same way you judge others, you will be judged, and with the measure you use, it will be measured to you."

Faithfulness: Proverbs 3:5–6, "Trust in the Lord with all your heart and lean not on your own understanding; in all your ways acknowledge Him and He will make your paths straight."

Fear: Romans 8:28, "We know that in all things God works for the good of those who love Him, who have been called according to His purpose."

Forgiveness: Colossians 3:13, "Bear with each other and forgive whatever grievances you may have against one another. Forgive as the Lord forgave you."

Future: Jeremiah 29:11, "'For I know the plans I have for you,' declares the Lord, 'plans to prosper you and not to harm you, plans to give you hope and a future.'"

Gossip: James 1:26, "If anyone considers himself religious and yet does not keep a tight rein on his tongue, he deceives himself and his religion is worthless."

Gratitude: Psalm 118:1, "Give thanks to the Lord, for He is good; His love endures forever."

Healthy habits: Matthew 26:41, "'Watch and pray so that you will not fall into temptation. The spirit is willing, but the flesh is weak.'"

Harmony: I Peter 3:8, "Live in harmony with one another; be sympathetic, love as brothers, be compassionate and humble."

Honesty: Psalm 34:13, "Keep your tongue from evil and your lips from speaking lies."

Hurt: Romans 5:3–5, "Not only so, but we also rejoice in our sufferings, because we know that suffering produces perseverance; perseverance, character; and character, hope. And hope does not disappoint us, because God has poured out His love into our hearts by the Holy Spirit, whom He has given us."

Integrity: Titus 2:7–8, "In everything set an example by doing what is good. In your teaching show integrity, seriousness and soundness of speech that cannot be condemned, so that those who oppose you may be ashamed because they have nothing bad to say about us."

Jealousy: Proverbs 14:30, "A heart at peace gives life to the body, but envy rots the bones."

Kindness: I Thessalonians 5:15, "Make sure nobody pays back wrong for wrong, but always try to be kind to each other and to everyone else."

Loneliness: Hebrews 13:5b, "'Never will I leave you; never will I forsake you.'"

Love: Galatians 5:14, "The entire law is summed up in a single command: *Love your neighbor as yourself.*"

Patience: I Thessalonians 5:14b, "Be patient with everyone."

Perspective: Proverbs 19:21, "Many are the plans in a man's heart, but it is the Lord's purpose that prevails."

Pride: Proverbs 13:10, "Pride only breeds quarrels, but wisdom is found in those who take advice."

Purpose: I Corinthians 10:31, "So whether you eat or drink or whatever you do, do it all for the glory of God."

Suffering: Romans 8:18, "I consider that our present sufferings are not worth comparing with the glory that will be revealed in us."

Tolerance: Colossians 3:12, "Therefore, as God's chosen people, holy and dearly loved, clothe yourselves with compassion, kindness, humility, gentleness and patience."

Trustworthiness: Proverbs 6:16–19, "There are six things the Lord hates, seven that are detestable to him: haughty eyes, a lying tongue, hands that shed innocent blood, a heart that devises wicked schemes, feet that are quick to rush into evil, a false witness who pours out lies, and a man who stirs up dissension among brothers."

Values: Galatians 5:22–23, "But the fruit of the Spirit is love, joy, peace, patience, kindness, goodness, faithfulness, gentleness, and self-control. Against such things there is no law."

Wisdom: II Peter 1:5–8, "For this very reason, make every effort to add to your faith goodness; and to goodness, knowledge; and to knowledge, self-control; and to self-control, perseverance; and to perseverance, godliness; and to godliness, mutual affection; and to mutual affection, love. For if you possess these qualities in increasing measure, they will keep you from being ineffective and unproductive in your knowledge of our Lord Jesus Christ."

Worry: Philippians 4:6–7, "Do not be anxious about anything, but in everything, by prayer and petition, with thanksgiving, present your requests to God. And the peace of God, which transcends all understanding, will guard your hearts and minds in Christ Jesus."

Looking back, I can see all the things God has done to protect and strengthen me throughout my life. He protected and sustained me. He has kept you safe too. Our limited lens fails to see all that He has done for us. I guess the hardships are easier to notice. Look for His love and grace in your life. It is infinite.

WHEN RELIGION COMES WITH HURT

"My faith rest not in what I am, or shall be, or feel, or know, but in what Christ is, in what he has done, and in what he is doing for me."

—CHARLES H. SPURGEON

In my years of Christian counseling, I didn't work exclusively with Christians. I also worked with those who did not believe in God and others who felt oppressed from religious experiences. When one has a hurtful experience with religion, it often leads to high sensitivity and avoidance of spiritual principles. I have listened to disturbing accounts from clients abused by religious leaders or family members whom they trusted, leaving them with confusion and anger toward God. If you had a negative experience in the past with a religious person who said or did hurtful things to you or a loved one, I know that this pain is real. Nothing I can say to you will make up for that hurt.

Despite the pain, you can heal and move forward, knowing that you did not ask for the hurt, but can manage the process of moving forward from it. God is not to blame for the unhealthy attitudes or behaviors of the authority figures who hurt you. The accountability lies with the offender of the spiritual wound, not with you or God Himself. God and religion are not the same. Religion is about practices. Your relationship with God belongs to you, and only you.

Anything that takes a negative hold on you, reinforcing your struggle, results in more hurt. By working through the pain, you will find freedom. Remember, if someone of faith has been hurtful, it comes from their backpack. It's not about you. Will you stop giving that experience power over you?

Many religious systems are founded on similar teachings. If you don't know what you believe or have hurts from experiences of your past, God can guide you. Accept the hurt. Know where it comes from. Ask questions. Read. Work through it. You don't have to keep carrying this anger around.

If you don't believe in God altogether, I am not here to convince you otherwise. Faith is believing without seeing. I don't have the power to change your mind. Only the Holy Spirit does. Faith is not something you can explain with logic. It is something you know with heartfelt certainty. I am blessed to have been given this faith by the Holy Spirit. I didn't earn it. I don't deserve it. But I have it. I trust God. He leads me.

I have always been a morning person. I recall getting up early as a child. My mother was always up before me. I would often find her at the kitchen table, reading her Bible or devotion book before anyone woke up. This memory and modeling taught me to prioritize faithfulness as a core value. This lesson has nurtured a value that stays in my backpack forever.

Mom's life has not been easy, but her faith has been unshakeable. God comes before everything else. Regardless of the many difficult hurts she has carried in her backpack, she moved through them with unwavering faith. Mom taught me this lifestyle habit. Her consistent spiritual strength is how I choose to carry my backpack too. Studying my Bible in quiet prayer and praise trains my mind in big-picture perspective, nurturing patience and gratitude along life's way. Faith gives peace to difficult moments. It provides comfort in fear. It gives endurance in the uncertainty. It is the reason for my joy.

Let go of any unresolved emotions connected to your hurt. Don't let this turn into resentment that poisons you. You don't have to carry it anymore. Set down your anger and hurt. Choose to break free.

FOR YOUR BACKPACK

When you know what belongs to God, you can learn to let go of worry and control. When you do, your backpack gets much lighter.

THE BACKPACK TOOLKIT

———

"It's not what you look at that matters, it's what you see."

—HENRY DAVID THOREAU

Regardless of cause, when people get stuck emotionally, they often exhibit similar patterns. I have observed unproductive thinking that infiltrates the mind, creating bodies tied up with tension, often leading to poor coping behaviors. When the body and mind are not in healthy regulation, self-care habits decline, negatively affecting well-being. In order to create new healthy pathways, you need tools that help you retrain old emotional habits. New ways of managing difficulties take time and practice. Over decades of providing therapy, I have developed a practical toolkit that is easy to learn and use.

The Wellness GPA incorporates skill areas (body, mind, and choice) to promote optimal well-being. The backpack toolkit includes visual images and easy-to-remember metaphors to nurture new habits in these three skill areas. Sometimes it takes the use of a few different tools to override your stubborn habits. Grab a notebook so that you can record these tools and answer the journal entries associated with them. As you carefully read through these tools, highlight the ones that are most useful for you. Practice them regularly to build new pathways for a healthier you!

What follows are: ten emotional tools for your body, ten cognitive tools for your mind, and ten behavioral tools for healthy living. I want these tools to live in your backpack from this day forward. I put this toolbox together for you to make it easier to reference in the book whenever you need to find a tool to help you. They have helped countless clients. I hope you adopt a few of them too, adding needed tools in your backpack.

10 EMOTION TOOLS FOR BODY BALANCE

Body balance tools help you reset the adrenaline imbalance that occurs from stress. Each of us processes information differently, impacting how we manage stress. There is not a right or wrong way to reset—only your way. When you know how to manage difficult moments, your emotions will feel more balanced and your body will function better.

TOOL 1
The Stoplight

The stoplight tool is helpful in situations where you notice a strong internal reaction to a triggered experience. For children and adults with strong reactions, this tool is extremely effective. It works exceptionally well with triggered anger. When emotion increases in intensity, picture in your mind coming to a stoplight. This image creates a pause that slows down emotion. The stoplight has three lights: red, yellow, and green. By doing this exercise, you practice regulating the trigger.

- *Red light* means stop. Sit down. Shift from your mind to your body. Actively direct stillness throughout your body.
- *Yellow light* slows and calms the body and the mind. Purposefully slow down with slow, diaphragmatic breathing (belly breathing), relaxing your muscles from head to toe, so that you calm your body before thinking through the situation carefully with intention. Slow your mind, like a train coming to a stop. Stay in that slowness for a few minutes. When your body and mind find harmony, you can examine the choices available to manage your situation based on your big-picture goal.
- *Green light* is your clear decision to move forward. This requires a calm and secure energy, executing the best solution aligned with your values and desired outcome. Execute your plan.

Certain personalities struggle with accepting problems, jumping to solutions too quickly because "negativity" makes them uncomfortable. This tool works great for them because addressing feelings is an important part of resolving problems. If you are at a stoplight, you can't just go because you want to. You need to stop and wait until it is safe to go. This tool helps those who don't like to stop and confront problems. Slowing down and creating emotional safety needs to happen before going forward with solutions. It respects other "drivers" who have feelings that need to be addressed.

Similarly, the green light signals drivers to go forward. If you have a habit of getting stuck on negativity (circling problems), this tool will help you stop and pause only briefly, reminding you to move forward quickly when the light changes. After you release your feelings and they are heard, shift forward quickly with intentional solutions.

By using "stoplight" language, you create an honest conversation about when to stop, slow down, and move forward with solutions. For example, if you are in a conflict with a partner, you can request a break when in a "redlight" moment, which cautions you to stop and slow down to gain perspective before entering solution talk. By naming it, you both have a signal for a reset break. When you are ready, let your partner know that you are now in the "greenlight" mindset. This shared language identifies when to take a break to manage emotions and when to come together to solve the problem.

TOOL 2
Servicing Your Vehicle–Lights on the Dashboard

When we need to take our vehicles in for maintenance, the dashboard lights up with indicators for the service needs that keep the car safe and working well. Our bodies do that too. We carry tension in our bodies when stress takes us off track. Notice when you are not managing emotion well. Imagine your body's internal dashboard lighting up in these poor regulation moments. Learning to recognize your body's signals alerts you to examine your needs carefully to manage a difficult situation. Your lights can be indicators for slowing down when upset or speeding up to create energy when your internal tank is low. You can get skilled at recognizing these indicators so you can reset.

Reflection questions for your internal dashboard:

- What situations create strong emotions for me?
- When do I find myself shut down and turned off emotionally?
- When do I end up in aimless busyness, ignoring the warning lights?
- What are the signs I need to talk through my feelings with someone?
- When am I shut down, avoiding talking through difficulties?
- What do my overreactive moments look like?

- When do I find myself using unhealthy coping skills to escape feelings?

If you can't answer these questions, then the best avenue is to talk it through with a counselor, developing a safe path to self-discovery and insight. Learning your body's signals helps you best understand what you need, just as the lights signal maintenance.

When stuck in energy imbalance, visualize dashboard lights. If you are without energy, picture your gas tank light flashing. In this moment, get moving to fill your tank with energy to accomplish the next task. If stuck in anxiety, picture your oil change light going on. This shifts you away from the trigger, recognizing that this is your reaction affecting your current functioning. Doing a quick "emotional oil change" may look like talking the issue out with a confidant, doing an act of self-care, or writing out what you need to do to solve the problem. It might be a slowing-down ritual to get clear on your big-picture intention. Recognizing your emotion lights helps you function well in stress, resulting in fewer maintenance problems!

TOOL 3
Backpack GPS

Just like understanding your dashboard, you need navigation tools. Whether you are walking or driving, you need to skillfully get to your destination.

When taking a road trip, you get in the driver's seat with your GPS map and a full tank of gas. If you jump into the back seat (or even worse, the trunk) you passively rely on others to get you there. Often in challenging moments, we unknowingly ride in the back seat with others driving us around. When we are trying to please others, rather than understanding our own needs, we are sitting in the wrong seat. We cannot properly navigate this way. Choose to be in the driver's seat by knowing what you want and need, directing this path with clarity. Don't just go along for the ride, looking passively out the window.

Your backpack holds your GPS device outlining the path you will take. The tank of gas is your self-care choices, which keep you at your full potential so you can handle roadblocks, construction, potholes, and unanticipated delays along the way. Your GPS system is created by your defined values and guides the direction of your hike. Defining these areas can help you in any problem situation. When you approach a roadblock in your day, ask yourself, "If I am operating from my best self, what will I do?"

If you are hiking with your backpack securely in place, you carry the fuel (food and drink) that keeps your energy high for the long hike. Your backpack also has a map of your hiking trail, so you know where you are going. Based on the difficulty of the hike, you may need extra supplies to sustain you. If you aimlessly walk along without following a map, you are likely to get lost. Executing a clear plan, noticing the scenery, and having what you need in your backpack makes the hike most pleasurable.

Following the rules of the park is key. You wouldn't litter or destroy your surroundings while on the hike, would you? Of course not. You protect the beauty. This is the compass of your hike led by your values (rules and guides) along the journey. What are the rules and guides to your life? Do you follow them even when you are upset? Wouldn't that help the challenging hikes go smoother?

TOOL 4
Observing the Cars Passing By

When it comes to strong emotion, the power of observation is the key to both awareness and regulation. You can't manage the situation if you are not observing what is happening inside and around you. As stated earlier, your danger zones are when you are blocking emotion or when you are overreacting, attaching to it.

A visual exercise taken from DBT is especially useful in heightened emotional moments. Think about walking alongside a busy road. You have your backpack securely fastened as you walk. If a speeding car goes by, you wouldn't panic, chase it, or run away. You wouldn't stop walking. Nor would you be angry that it passed by, throwing items from your backpack at the moving vehicle. Furthermore, you wouldn't pretend that you didn't see it. Instead, you would observe it, watching it go by. When our bodies are triggered to emotions like anger or anxiety, you can do that same thing. In those difficult moments, you can watch the feeling travel past you, like a vehicle passing by. Some triggering events are big like semitrucks and RVs. Others are small like motorcycles or runners. Regardless of the size of the trigger, stay committed to walking the path confidently. This keeps you on your path moving forward.

Identify the triggers you need to observe so that you are not reacting with strong emotion. When you make this list, they will be the cars that simply pass by!

TOOL 5
The Sleep Ritual for the Well-Rested Traveler

When we travel and need to navigate a long journey, it is important to be well rested. If you embark on a long hike, but didn't sleep well the night before, you may not enjoy the hike fully. Sleep is imperative to mood. It is necessary for our functioning. Having a sleep routine keeps the body and mind functioning optimally. A sleep ritual is a soothing collection of habits you follow to prepare for sleeping well. Transitioning from activity to peacefulness retrains your body to prepare for sleep, especially after a habit of wakefulness has been established.

A sleep ritual might look like one of these options:

- Reading for twenty minutes, a warm shower, dim lights, a cup of tea, and then prayer time.
- Putting on pj's, shutting down screen time, writing your gratitude list, and doing a sleep meditation.
- Tidying up your home, writing a journal reflection for tomorrow's intention, and relaxing while reading with soft music playing in the background.

Your sleep ritual needs to reflect your needs and preferences. Shutting the brain down before sleep is necessary to quality health. Practice this ritual for as long as it takes to set the new pattern. Many give up on it before the habit pattern is set. Don't give up until it works.

Stress impacts sleep significantly. Late-night activity keeps your energy high, affecting how you transition to sleep. If you are in a high-stress season, choose to make sleep your priority. Set a consistent time for sleep. Perform a ritual that retrains your body to relax, shutting down thoughts to enjoy the peace that comes with the dark comfort of nighttime.

If you find yourself lying in bed awake, relax your muscles, scanning your body from head to toe. Feel your body against the sheets of your bed. Picture lights on in the different parts of your body, traveling from one part to another, shutting off each light. Shift from your mind to your body. Your thoughts can get in the way of your sleep by keeping track of the passing time or pulling you to an anxious place that anticipates being tired the next day. If you can't sleep, you can still rest peacefully, if this is your intention. The well-rested traveler is happier than the one who is exhausted. Peaceful rest is a habit that brings long-term rewards. Good sleep hygiene needs to be practiced over and over before habits change.

TOOL 6
Superpower Emotions

When it comes to any emotion (yes, any), it can be your superpower. We seldom think about emotion from this perspective. Most of the time when a client shares their struggle with negative emotion, they look at it as a weakness or burden.

Emotions help us understand our needs and the needs of others. We get stuck in attaching to labels, lacking awareness about what is going on internally. For example, if you habitually tell yourself you are depressed, it may not be accurate or helpful. Examine specifically what you are feeling. It may be loneliness, disappointment, hurt, or boredom, but your habit is to think that you are once again depressed. By sitting with emotion, you can observe it more carefully, breaking the pattern of seeing it as your identity. I have heard clients report emotion in vague terms.

Not helpful: "I am depressed!" Helpful: "I feel sad today. I want to isolate."

Not helpful: "I am a mess!" Helpful: "I am feeling scattered in my mind."

Not helpful: "I am miserable!" Helpful: "I feel apprehension and restlessness."

Not helpful: "I am not like others!" Helpful: "I feel uneasy about
_____."

Emotion can feel like a burden when not managed. In its strongest capacity, emotion brings amazing benefits to experience. For example, when anxiety is regulated, it brings energy, empathy, and carefulness. When anxiety takes over, it escalates insecurity and irrational fear, leading to outcome-seeking control behavior. Even anger can be a superpower. When regulated skillfully, it can point you to values you are passionate about, bringing clarity to your expectation. When anger is not regulated, it blocks and shreds closeness. Guilt is an emotion that can bring thoughtfulness and a strong conscience. Without it we would not learn from our mistakes, blocking the lessons that come from error. When not regulated, guilt nurtures fear and can lead to shame. This premise can be true for any emotion. When managed, it provides gifts. When not, it creates a struggle.

Our habits direct us to avoid uncomfortable feelings. In these moments we block emotion with positivity. We don't need to be positive all the time because this paradigm is unrealistic, often resulting from discomfort around emotion. Needing to feel happy all the time can lead to false positivity, which avoids real emotion. Resistance with addressing emotion pushes people away with feelings of not being heard in moments of pain. Dismissing emotion can lead to disorder, just as letting emotion control you escalates problems. Remember, the goal is to manage your feelings skillfully. This requires noticing it, accepting it, and using it to grow.

Understanding the dual nature of emotion encourages focus on regulation rather than on the mere presence of it. When emotion surfaces, begin by naming it accurately. Next, observe it like you notice the temperature in your car that needs adjusting when it is hot or cold outside. If your car sits outside in the weather elements, you expect to modify the temperature in your vehicle to create the comfort you need for driving. Expect to do that with emotion, observing it and moving it to the place of balance that brings you to your healthy self.

When my daughters were young, they loved the movie *The Incredibles*. They would talk about which superpower they wished they possessed. If speed were your superpower, you'd move so fast that time would seldom be a problem. If not managed well, this superpower could create all kinds of challenges. Going too fast, you might miss the beauty along the way, losing sight of what is happening around you. All our superpower emotions require regulation. Recognizing both sides of their functioning keeps you in your middle ground regulation zone. Your feelings deserve to be named and managed carefully like superpowers.

TOOL 7

The 4 Ms of Anxiety Management

Anxiety is common. Often portrayed as weakness, it is misunderstood. I observe some experiencing it as irritation, frustration, and anger that leads to negative control behaviors. Others experience it as worry, sadness, guilt, and self-doubt. Anxiety leads to a tight body feeling with surges of adrenaline that trigger negative thoughts. Anxiety can be mild, moderate, or even extreme. When extreme, it can lead to obsessive, intrusive thoughts as well as paralyzing fears and panic. Regardless of intensity, these four Ms are useful guides to managing anxiety.

Your Anxiety Managers:

1. *Meditation*—letting go of fears and insecurities through prayer or a ritual of calming the mind through peaceful thoughts and a sensory soothing experience.
2. *Mindfulness*—the practice of noticing when you are not emotionally present, reconnecting to your sensory environment, observing thoughts, and creating intention in the moment.
3. *Muscle Relaxation*—relaxing each part of the body, releasing stored tension.
4. *Movement*—when the mind goes into a loop, getting up and moving to shift from mind to body, stopping the loop.

Like any other emotion, when anxiety spirals, the mind loops. By practicing these techniques, you can pivot from old habits to new, regulated ones. Anxiety is not a curse. It is a gift that gives you wisdom later. You can learn to treat it that way.

TOOL 8
Your Sensory Toolbox

When you are building a home or fixing it up, a toolbox is needed. Each tool has a function that can be used in making or repairing something broken. Your sensory toolbox is used the same way. Your senses come in seven different forms. They are identified by sight, hearing, smell, taste, touch, movement, and body position.

Identify soothing activities you can use to manage your response to strong emotion. Identifying environmental items can be grounding and resetting for triggered emotion.

- *Visual*: What do you see around you? Choose something that carries meaning.
- *Auditory*: What do you hear? Focus on a soothing sound.

- *Olfactory*: What do you smell? Absorb yourself in the pleasurable smell.
- *Gustatory*: What can you taste? Take a small, savoring bite of something you love.
- *Tactile*: Touch or hold something of meaning. What item provides this comfort?
- *Vestibular*: Find movement that helps to restore balance. Sitting upright, standing, or walking mindfully can pivot the trigger.
- *Proprioception*: This is the body awareness sense, informing us where our body parts are relative to each other. It gives us direction about how much force to use in movement (such as handling a delicate flower that needs a gentle touch). What items or activities require this sensitive movement?

This sensory toolbox works exceptionally well with children. When they have a toolbox of sensory soothing activities available to them in emotional moments, they develop skills for calming down when they are overreacting. Helping them create a feelings toolbox kit teaches them to work through emotions, a needed skill for later difficulties. Direct them to use it in reactive moments.

TOOL 9
Your Remote Control

When your emotions escalate, visualize a remote control made specifically for you. This remote control can change the channel, lower or raise your volume, and utilize different modes for optimal use. Remotes can record; you can go back and watch programming that you missed. They also have a delete function to get rid of old stories that you no longer need.

When emotions get loud, you can use these functions internally to regulate your emotional experience. This impacts the big picture in your relationships with others. Taking a moment to use your internal remote control is useful when you realize the moment you can turn the channel, lower volume, or delete programming.

By going back and reviewing later, when operating from a place of calm, you can create clarity and bring closeness. We all have an internal remote allowing us to manage any situation effectively. Knowing when and how to use your internal remote creates direction during difficult programming.

Functions of your remote:

- *Volume*: Turn it up when you are shut down and avoiding conversation. Turn it down when you feel yourself escalating.
- *Channel*: When your reactions become unhelpful, change the channel and shift to a station that creates peace.
- *Delete*: Delete unhelpful stories that pull you away from managing emotions. Notice when these stories are playing so you can hit the delete button.
- *Rewind*: Go back to conversations when you are calm so that you can say things productively. You can do that with yourself and with others.
- *Pause*: Take a pause when you need it. Don't power through a difficult situation. Ask for a break to think it through from a helpful perspective.
- *Power*: Hit the power button when you know you need self-care. Shutting down intentionally for the benefit of reset is essential to good mental health.

You might have more or different keys on your remote. Using this visual imagery tool allows you to shift gears in emotional situations. What buttons are on your remote?

TOOL 10

Body Language—Listening to Your Body When It Speaks

Your body talks to you when you are stressed out with pain and tension. As you gain skills in body awareness, you will start to notice this more. Your body might speak to you with experiences such as a headache, tightness in your chest, stomach or colon discomfort, tension, or fatigue. When anxiety is present, it becomes comfortable living in your body in various places. Listening to your body is necessary to managing it.

Medical issues are often connected to emotional patterns in the body. In moments when your body is holding tension or pain, take time to relax the distressed area. Gently place your hand where you feel pain residing. You need to learn to notice, soothe the pain, and let it pass by rather than fearing it. Fear creates rumination about why the stress is there. Be careful not to get hung up on "the why." What you do about it matters more.

In moments when your body is signaling pain, ask yourself these reflective questions:

- What part of my body is under stress right now?
- What am I feeling? Name the emotion(s) specifically. Be careful of general labels such as "I am depressed." When you see yourself as a disorder, it owns you.
- How can I best soothe this area of my body, releasing or managing the pain?
- What is my body saying to me right now? How can I honor it?

Your body holds the map to your emotion. By learning to understand body and emotion simultaneously, you develop roads for regulating stress. When your body talks, listen and comfort it so that you don't escape into a habit that keeps that distress going. If you struggle with chronic pain, whether physical or emotional, this awareness is essential.

10 COGNITIVE TOOLS FOR SETTING THE MIND
TOOL 1
THINK First!

Before you speak,

THINK

T – is it **TRUE?**

H – is it **HELPFUL?**

I – is it **INSPIRING?**

N – is it **NECESSARY?**

K – is it **KIND?**

At Delta, we use the THINK FIRST framework for governing mindset. It is a common map in many school classrooms for guiding both thoughts and conversation. I crossed this information on the internet years ago, making a sign for my clinical office to remember it as my personal guide and teaching device. It is a mindset tool that reduces side talk and gossip, which helps us prevent violations to our company values. This tool is great for promoting a healthy family culture, as well as a personal map for friendship.

Before you decide if what you are thinking is accurate, assess it based on the THINK acronym. Before speaking sensitive information to others, use it as a guide! Is what you are thinking or feeling actually *true*? Is it *helpful* to you and others involved? Does it *inspire* and build others up? Is it *necessary* to focus on? Is it *kind*? This thoughtful acronym is an easy way to catch thinking and communication errors quickly.

This acronym will help you retrain your inner critic voice, creating alignment with the values of your best self. It directs you to slow down and think first!

TOOL 2
ANTs (Automatic Negative Thoughts)

I recall reading Daniel Amen's children's book *Mind Coach* to former young therapy clients. He had written about negative thoughts using the term ANTs (automatic negative thoughts), and this image stuck with me. It gave a visualization of thoughts like an infestation of creepy-crawly bugs that we can exterminate.

I remember taking my young clients on imaginary picnics to teach this concept. I would ask them what to do if they discovered ants all over our picnic blanket.

They would typically say:

- "Step on them!"

- "Shake them off!"
- "Flip the blanket over and sit on the other side."

I quickly agreed. This act of exterminating the ants makes the picnic more enjoyable. When you notice ANTs in your mind, get rid of them. Step on them. Shake them off. Life can be a picnic if you let it. Others will enjoy being with you more.

ANTs can be overgeneralizing or minimizing difficult situations, jumping to an angry mindset, feeling sorry for yourself, or taking unintended situations personally. Recognizing negative thoughts helps you enjoy your life and those around you more. I often called them angry negative thoughts or anxious negative thoughts based on the themes shared by clients.

Here are some common ANTs that I have taught others to retrain:

- "I am so tired today, but it will pass. I have managed this before." This is healthier than repeatedly circling, "I am just so tired!"
- "I am going to manage this situation by taking a walk at lunch to reset!" Saying this is more productive than saying, "I am so stressed out!"
- "This is what I am striving to get done today." Watch out for saying, "I can't do more than I am already doing."
- "I choose to do _____. This is the best option for me." This thought connects you toward choice rather than ruminating on a feeling such as: "no one understands."
- "That guy was reacting with strong anger." This thought is healthier than: "that guy was a total moron!"

Make a list of your ANTs to notice them quickly and shake them off when they infest your mind. When you are looking for them, you will see them. Until you do, they will live in your head!

TOOL 3
Mind Mazes and Land Mines

Oftentimes our brains work like mind maze puzzles. When I was a young girl, I loved the maze books where I could practice finding the correct path to the treasure chest. Sometimes our brains work like these complicated mazes. Thinking about an event from twenty different angles can lead to feeling exhausted and confused about what to do next. If this sounds familiar, you might have thoughts circling "the what ifs", "the whys", "the shoulds," and "the worst-case scenarios." These ANTs lead to fear and insecurity.

For example, if you have social anxiety and are invited to a social event, you may start to review the negative possibilities that talk you out of going. This mind maze adds to your anxiety, reinforcing an old pattern of fearing potential bad outcomes. When you recognize being in your thinking maze, you can direct yourself out. As a rule of thumb, doing what makes you grow is better than reviewing what could go wrong.

Overthinking can be just as harmful as not thinking at all. It steals your time and energy. When you overthink situations, it is like stepping on land mines in your head, blowing up your mood. This can lead to justifying unnecessary control or escape behaviors. Know the thinking land mines that blow up your mood. Identify them so you stay on solid ground. With your backpack on, take the path that leads you straight toward your goal, avoiding the dangerous spots that slow you down.

TOOL 4
Pop-Ups and Jack-in-the-Boxes

We all experience thoughts that make us uncomfortable. In moments of extreme emotion, your mind can create intrusive thoughts that trigger fear or shame. The content of these dark thoughts can differ for each person. They can be angry, sexual, panic-driven, or shameful. When this occurs, I have two images that come to mind.

- *Jack-in-the-box:* When intrusive thoughts occur, imagine a jack-in-the-box toy. I am befuddled by the creation of this toy, designed to frighten children. Creepy music plays and when you are not expecting it, the scary clown pops out. When the clown scares you, you close the lid, placing it back in the box. Scary thoughts work the same way. You can choose to shut down any thought that becomes a habit if you decide it is not serving you. This is a cognitive retraining process. With your intrusive thoughts, tell yourself, "That was a scary thought. I will not give power to it." When you give positive or negative energy to any thought, over time it will automate. Pay attention to shutting down the thought, not fearing it.
- *Computer virus pop-ups:* Because of the complex nature of our minds, we often have thought "pop-ups" that we can learn to spot. These thoughts are inconsistent with our values and our best self. When you begin to watch for them, you will see them. When you notice them, consider them as viral computer ads that pop up on the screen of your electronic device. You can "x" out of those thoughts quickly, not giving them attention to grow or develop into an emotional virus that spins you out of control in panic.

TOOL 5
Self-Talk Mantras and Affirmations

When it comes to difficult situations, we all carry different beliefs in our backpacks. A mantra is a phrase or saying that brings you back on track when your self-talk spirals negatively. When our kids were young, we used to tell them that Schneider meant "never give up."

As they faced difficult challenges, we would reinforce that mantra, returning them to productive thinking. When I am faced with a challenge, I use my personal mantra "whatever you pay attention to grows." This helps me get clear with what I am choosing to focus on in the situation. Do you have a favorite quote or saying that does this for you? If you don't, you should adopt one. Use it as a guide when challenges are before you. Then share it with others to spread the wisdom.

When our self-talk becomes negative, we see ourselves inaccurately, attaching to the belief that something is wrong with us. Instead, we can learn to notice the emotion connected to the negative thought, letting it pass by rather than attaching to it. Take for example the thought: "I am so dumb! Why can't I figure this out?" This thought attaches stupidity to your belief about yourself. This is not helpful in the least! Instead, say in your mind, "I am noticing that I am feeling dumb right now. I am not dumb, but everyone feels this way sometimes." This healthier response is a pivot away from *becoming* the feeling. Notice the feeling, don't personalize it. It leads to a false sense of self.

Assess these differences:

- Attaching: "I am depressed." Noticing: "I am feeling sad and tired right now. This will pass if I get moving."
- Attaching: "I can't do this." Noticing: "I am feeling like I can't do this, which isn't true."
- Attaching: "He is a jerk!" Noticing: "I am feeling angry because of his tone with me right now."
- Attaching: "She is a brat!" Noticing: "I am frustrated about her disrespectful behavior."

Affirmation mantras can correct negative self-talk that derails how you see yourself and others. Our "in the moment" feelings are not the same as our true beliefs about ourselves and others. Affirmations begin with "I am" and end with your behavioral intention. For example, I have an affirmation mantra that keeps me exercising. In the past I have falsely viewed myself as an unathletic person. Writing this statement helped me work through my mindset block. When I get up in the morning, I say to myself: *"Holly, you are a physically fit, healthy woman who values taking care of the body God has given to you. I choose to work out and be active today."* This active intention leads me toward my goal. When I am not in the mood to exercise, I have to be aware of my desire to attach to my old thought that says, "I hate working out. I am not good at this!" When I notice my habit thought rising, observe my initial feeling of resistance, and override it with my affirmation, I honor my intention. You can do this too! Write your affirmation today. It will replace old thoughts that no longer lead you.

TOOL 6
Turtle Insecurities

What are the thoughts that make you feel emotionally stuck? Take a moment to write down a list of anxiety-provoking thoughts. These are your "turtle" thoughts that stop your ability to operate from your best self. Thoughts must be helpful and intentional, or they will create anxiety. Any negative thought can be flipped over to become productive. I call this method flipping: the turtle.

Visualize each negative thought like a turtle laying on its back, unable to go anywhere. This pairing image is a reminder that we are vulnerable to disaster when we are stuck. Practicing the technique of making thoughts productive by flipping them to a productive message allows you to look at any given situation in the best possible way. Every insecurity has a secure counterpart that provides healing to an unproductive thought.

Here are some examples:

- Turtle: "No one understands me." Flipped: "For people to understand me, I must be clear and calm, knowing what I want and why I want it."
- Turtle: "I can't figure this out." Flipped: "I will take a break and come back to this problem with fresh eyes. I am capable and determined to accomplish my goal."
- Turtle: "If I tell the truth, people will hate me." Flipped: "Telling the truth in kindness and love is the best version of me. I choose faith over fear."
- Turtle: "I avoid difficult situations because they give me anxiety." Flipped: "I will lean into the discomfort and work through it, so I can grow."
- Turtle: "I can't manage my emotions." Flipped: "I am learning how to observe and regulate these situations. With practice comes mastery."

Practice flipping your turtle thoughts over. You can flip any negative thought! If you don't, you will remain stuck like a turtle on its back, going absolutely nowhere.

TOOL 7
Code Words

Words are powerful. They can make or break a conversation. Code words can be words that signal a need for reset. They can be used to help you pivot in a challenging situation. If used in relationships, code words can mutually bring you to a neutral place. Applying a code word in a frustrating moment provides a needed pause to reflect or creates intention when communication goes south.

Code words can create helpful space to slow down and rethink. When bookmarked briefly (mutually taking space before revisiting the topic), parties can gain perspective after a peaceful rebalance. Stopping a conversation until emotions are calm nurtures healthy resolve.

We socialized with a couple years ago who used to say "paper clip" when they were frustrated with each other. This was their code word to table a discussion and circle back at another time to prevent escalation. I found this particular code word interesting and useful. If used correctly, a paper clip brings materials together. If used improperly, it could be a weapon. Intention matters. Words hold powerful meaning. Code words can honor prediscussed plans and keep you accountable. They are helpful in parenting, marriage, and professional situations when emotions escalate.

Code words work great with children when you are in a public place and want to honor a confidential behavioral plan you created together.

TOOL 8
Your Alter Ego Personality

We all have an alter ego that gets in the way of our wellness. You might have an angry reactive personality in conflict or one that shuts down and avoids issues when life gets stressful. When anxiety is active, people circle topics repeatedly, escalating emotion.

At the core of conflict lies fear. I teach others to look inside, observing moments when their best self and their negative habit self holds power over their mindset. When it comes to these parts of self, I have suggested that clients name their inner critic voice that leads them astray. Naming this part of self can be useful in practicing the coaching conversation dialogue between your best self and your habit self that needs to be kept in check.

I referred to my unhelpful alter ego as "Negative Nellie." (I recall sharing with you my deep love for *Little House on the Prairie*; Nellie was a character on the show who frequently caused trouble.) Nellie gets in my way; she sees problems rather than solutions. She tends to notice all the worst-case scenarios that could go wrong, rather than focusing on what is going right or the solutions to make it right. She encourages me to say "no" in my default mode so that I can attach to the fear of uncertainty. When she leads me, I operate from insecurity, which leads to resisting things that are good for me. Nellie diminishes healthy risks that push my emotional growth. I watch out for her. She is a pain in my ass and does not get to be the boss of me! Sometimes she sneaks into my backpack and I have to remove her again.

What is the name of the alter ego that you will remove from your backpack? Give that difficult side of your personality a name you won't forget. Then keep watch so you shut down that problematic voice quickly. Don't let it be the boss in your head distorting your reality.

TOOL 9
The Wellness Journal Practice

When I would facilitate mental health groups, I regularly suggested that clients keep a wellness journal. This is a compilation of positive writing that helps you retrain your thinking for moments of heightened emotion.

Many clients journal ineffectively. When you pour out negative thoughts over and over, it can reinforce the insecurities surrounding emotions. Journaling needs to be productive with a purpose of understanding and retraining negative thoughts and emotions that fuel insecurity.

A wellness journal can incorporate:

- Personal values
- Positive memories of your past
- Your strengths
- Helpful change goals and action plans
- Affirmations
- Change mantras
- Intentional self-care plans
- Retrained thoughts
- Reset rituals
- Inspirational quotes, passages, or writing pieces
- Personal resilience stories

Over time, the writing in your journal becomes your consistent voice in times of trouble. I encourage you to do this for one year, recording your inspiration and tracking your growth. Down the line, you might decide to pass this book of wisdom to someone in need. It can be the voice of your backpack that inspires others. You can create a journal for developing gratitude, wisdom, leadership, parenting, or any growth area you want to expand. Name your journal after the strength you are building. Keep it close by so you can write and reflect daily.

I frequently share this Malcolm X quote: "When I is replaced by we, illness becomes wellness." Your contract with yourself is an important contract to uphold. Stay out of illness habits, which nurture disorder. Instead honor your relationship with your best self by consistently nurturing well-being habits. Your wellness journal will keep you on track with this goal!

TOOL 10
The Focus Zone

I think we can all relate to moments when our focus becomes problematic. Few people can say they never struggle with distraction. It is so common because our brain is always moving and firing. How do we expand our focus? Our mindset is key when creating an operating zone. By pairing a mindset with a soothing sensory experience, we can develop focus zones for optimal functioning.

When my youngest daughter was younger, she used to march around our kitchen island singing her "pump up" songs to prepare for her basketball games. I would laugh as she sang her eighties hair band music while getting in her "game zone." I taught her about this zone early in life to minimize the distraction in her extremely active mind.

When I decided to write this book, I created a focus zone for productivity. A few months into the process, my husband asked me why Enya was our top Spotify artist. I chuckled and responded, "Well dear, she helps me write." Establishing a consistent writing ritual, I used sensory tools to create an environment conducive to focus. By lighting my candle and listening to Enya's playlist, I would say to myself, "It's focus time; you got this, girl!" I had to do this repeatedly in order to make this technique effective. Most tools do not work because people do not practice them long enough to automate the habit.

While in college, my daughters used this same approach to optimize their study habits. It can work for reducing test anxiety, and many of my clients use the approach when preparing for certification exams required for their job. It can work if you are procrastinating on any task.

In a nutshell, when you need to focus, create a Body-Mind-Choice ritual:

1. Create a soothing sensory experience activating your senses (sounds, smell, vision, taste, or touch).
2. Pair this experience with a focus mindset in your self-talk (such as "This is my focus zone. I will be productive!").
3. Practice the pairing over and over until the zone creates automated focus (typically thirty days of practice, unless you have a stubborn brain, then do it longer).

10 BEHAVIORAL TOOLS FOR HEALTHY LIVING
TOOL 1
Decision Buckets

Decision buckets can be used in almost any situation and with any age or population. Anytime you are struggling in your thoughts about what to do, the buckets can direct decision-making. By breaking your dilemma into three choices, you stop worrying about negative outcomes and address your best choice. This is how it works. Picture three buckets ranging from small to large next to each other.

- Small bucket: "let it go" choice
- Medium bucket: "do your part" solution
- Large bucket: "follow your plan" method

The *small* bucket is for little problems that need not require your energy. Rate your problem using a ten-scale. If the issue is below a four on the importance scale, you need not figure out what to do. The "let it go" bucket directs you to quickly release insignificant worries or frustrations. This small bucket includes difficult situations, not patterned problems. Directing yourself to "let it go" creates a quick habit of not getting easily stirred up.

Small bucket items include:

- Noticing a rude person while driving or out in your community
- Momentary errors
- A negative attitude from someone who is typically in a good mood
- An irritation that is an exception to the norm
- Delays or pivots around unimportant events
- Daily things that are out of your control
- Resolved situations from the past

The "let it go" bucket keeps your backpack light, so you don't use it like a junk drawer!

The *medium* bucket is for problematic patterns that require a solution. These are situations that continue to arise, requiring more than a quick discard. Using similar scoring, they are moderate in size, typically affecting you between a four and seven on the problem ten-scale. Because they are repetitive in nature, these problems require a specific solution on your end.

A good example of a medium bucket item is a repetitive interaction pattern that is offensive in your relationship. It is not an isolated bad mood, but a pattern of interactions that requires a conversation for understanding and solution. Talking through this unhelpful pattern in your relationship may be the solution you seek. The "do my part" bucket choice encourages you to open up and solve the problem quickly, rather than waiting for months or years, causing resentment and anger.

Examples include:

- Communication patterns that need adjusting
- Work protocols that need improving
- Friendship irritation patterns that can be resolved simply
- Small parenting issues that arise, needing solutions

The *large* "follow your plan" bucket is for problems that are not going to be solved with a conversation or one-time solution. This bucket directs you to accept that the problem is big enough to require a systematic plan to follow and practice over time. This bucket often involves the help of another person for systematic change.

Big bucket examples include:

- Starting counseling for personal or relationship unhappiness
- Changing a lifestyle issue (like necessary weight loss)
- Recovery from a health issue
- Grief or loss
- Working through heavy emotional pain from a life transition
- Panic attacks, depression, or pervasive disorders that linger

Each of these items require an extended process that needs a patient and systematic plan. When you direct yourself toward choice you can drop that issue in the correct bucket and execute resolve. Know your buckets and use them to organize your boundaries.

TOOL 2
Wrap the Bleeding Wound First

When we hurt, we easily become defensive. When defenses are heightened, the other person involved in the conflict reacts to your negative energy, either fighting back or pulling away. If you are self-aware, you step back realizing that when someone is hurt, you tend to the wound before you create solutions or address your needs. Emotional wounds are like physical ones. Tending to the wound first directs the energy for healing.

If something creates an emotional bleed, take time to soothe the wound before addressing the cause or solution. We do this with empathy messages and self-soothing habits, which de-escalate emotion. Likewise, when you are in the presence of someone who is hurting, give emotional space to "calm the wound" before discussing it. Watch out for defensiveness, which creates injury on top of injury. By setting a calm mindset before leaning in, you stop the bleeding emotions and mutually solve the problem. When you do this systematically, closeness occurs, creating deeper connection around sensitive topics.

Difficulties occur when we get stuck on a problem or when we gloss over it too quickly because it makes us uncomfortable to talk about it. That would be like seeing a wound as life-threatening when it isn't or pretending that the wound is not there when it is. Choose to address the wound properly so that recovery is smooth.

- Ignoring the wound: *"Everything will be fine. Stop worrying about this!"*
- Focusing on the wound: *"I can't believe this happened. This is awful. We will never recover from this."*
- Wrapping the wound: *"Tell me how this is affecting you. How can I help so we can get through this together?"*

This extra step is a healing energy to any difficult situation. Clean the wound before putting the bandage on!

TOOL 3
Talking Temperature

This temperature tool is the *how-to* method for communicating around sensitive topics. Giving your most helpful energy motivates change. Energy often dictates the direction of a challenging moment. The temperatures include:

- Hot: irritable and angry, sarcasm, defensive tone
- Cold: emotionally distant, shut down, apathetic, or ignoring the issue
- Warm: inviting energy, gentle, and accountable

Whenever we communicate our needs, it should come from authentic warmth. If you are not able to speak your truth in love and kindness, you have work to do inside of yourself before sharing your perspective. Take time to recenter emotionally before leaning back in. Skilled communication is consistently warm. Any cold or hot energy will shut down the connection. When your temperature changes in conversation, own it and request a break. Your temperature sets the tone for how you lead. Warmth is the energy that makes the hike most pleasurable. Keep it warm, please!

TOOL 4
Communication Styles

Awareness of the four primary styles of communication belongs in your backpack. The imagery in these four types will keep you on track with your behavior.

> *Bulldozer:* aggressive, harsh communication; running over someone else with your words without empathy or a helpful tone.

Each of us knows a bulldozer communicator. Who are the people in your life who give you this feeling of being flattened by their words, tone, or agenda? If you walk away from someone and feel like they just ran over you, stand up for yourself. If you are the person who bulldozes, stop doing that, please.

Doormat: passive communication, holding feelings in, and avoiding honesty about how you feel.

Anxiety tends to be high in those who are passive. They often want to say how they feel but don't because of the uncertainty about how it will turn out. Passive behavior is disrespectful to the self and to the person you are holding back on. It is a lie creating an unhealthy cover story. Don't do that. Be open about your feelings. Be kind. Tell the truth. You and others can handle it.

Back window: indirect communication or behavior, letting others know you are upset but refusing to talk about it constructively.

This passive-aggressive method is an indirect way of communicating your needs. Instead of saying how you feel directly, you act it out in a way for the other person to observe. Manipulation and guilt messages are often involved in this type of communication. The silent treatment also belongs in this category. Acting angrily, using sarcasm, or withdrawing from the conversation fall into this approach. Be direct. Don't play games. Nobody benefits from mind games.

Front door communication: respectful, calm, and direct conversation about how you feel; being accountable for how to fairly get your needs met. This is done by asking calmly to talk through an issue respectfully, like knocking on the door before entering.

If you have good manners, you wouldn't barge into the home of another. Out of respect, you would knock before entering. Communication with all parties, regardless of comfort in the relationship, deserves this respect.

The "knock first" method looks like this:

- "Do you mind if we talk about _____? I want to get on the same page with you."
- "I have been thinking about _____ lately. Do you have time to process this with me?"
- "I would like to share my feelings on _____. When you are in a good headspace, can we sit down and resolve this?"
- "I am puzzled by _____. I would love to exchange feedback and perspective."

Please knock and enter respectfully. It honors the relationship and represents you in your best communication.

TOOL 5
3 Rs of Healthy Habit Living

The three Rs (rules, routines, and rituals) can be used for almost any goal you want to change in your life. The three areas become your plan of intention. Using them can jump-start a project or help with a lifestyle change. By defining all three areas, you create a plan that would allow you to change an unhealthy pattern. This works especially well with life transition changes.

- *Rules*: defining expectations and specific boundaries for healthy living
- *Routines*: consistent structure that supports boundaries
- *Rituals*: mini routines or patterns of functioning that are built into your habits

For example, if you have a conflict with a co-parent over how to manage your child's behavior, create a plan for each of these areas to increase continuity between homes. When rules, routines, and rituals are clearly defined and understood, you focus on keeping the structure rather than the problem itself.

When it comes to parenting, the three Rs teach children emotional skills for independence and self-mastery. If you are a parent who rescues your child from difficulty, you are stealing the skills they need to learn to be healthy risk-takers in the future. Honoring rules and routines helps children trust themselves so that they don't need to rely on you for everything. As a parent, stop feeling for them and "saving the day" when pain shows up. Teach your child to handle pain by sitting in it, understanding it, and working through it.

If you are a new empty nester, focus your efforts on the three Rs, which will help you transition easier. This tool is useful for any personal or professional transition you are managing.

TOOL 6
3 As of Conflict

When it comes to conflict of any kind, the three As can get you from conflict to resolve. This is a tool that you can use in disciplinary moments with your child or after an argument with a friend or family member. It is the perfect formula to follow after an emotional meltdown or anger outburst. When we model accountability, we create connection and learning in a difficult situation. Follow these steps when it is time to process through a problem that has occurred.

1. *Admit* the mistake. Be specific about what you did wrong.
2. *Apologize* sincerely for hurting feelings and for the error. Be clear about what you did wrong, without "buts" or excuses.

3. *Amend* for the future by saying what you will do better next time. Be specific and clear about the lesson learned and why the change is important.

I used this formula regularly for teachable moments following disciplinary correction. This backpack tool can be used as a map for resolving any misunderstanding or conflict you have with people in your life.

TOOL 7
LEAD, Not Please

Communication should not be about pleasing the other person at your expense. When we are caught up in pleasing others, we stop leading. Helpful communication is about managing your life based on your values and needs. If you use the LEAD tool (listen with energy, accountability, and decisions), it directs you clearly.

L: Listen to understand, asking questions for clarity and reflecting to be sure you understand fully.

E: Use warm *energy* as your tone prevents escalation or shut down, which are barriers to resolving problems.

A: Be *accountable* for your part, avoiding blame language and keeping score because it causes division.

D: Mutually beneficial *decisions* give all who are involved a fair and equitable solution.

Too often we become passive in conversations, reacting instead of leading. You can practice directing conflict from misunderstanding to clarity. Look for the "*and*" in the situation, rather than the "*or.*"

When we get stuck in black-and-white thinking, we forget to consider the best option, which is seeing the solution in both polarities.

For example, ask yourself, "Should I back down or stand my ground?" Mutually beneficial decisions use an "*and*" perspective. This means backing down on certain pieces that aren't as important to you, while at the same time holding your ground on important ones. The conversation does not need to be a conflict, but rather a win for both parties. You can be both skillful *and* assertive all rolled into one. Be an "*and*," not an "*or*"!

TOOL 8
R&R–Release and Reset

When you are emotionally stuck, whether in a moment of high stress or low energy, observing your "stuck" pattern is useful. Too often you hang onto stress, carrying it around with you all day, not realizing the impact it has on you. It often leads to muscle pain, tension headaches, fatigue, and mood changes. By recognizing your momentary imbalance, you can guide yourself to release it and reset back to balance. Acknowledging stress helps you create a choice to intentionally release the negative energy through a productive activity (such as taking a walk, journaling, reading, or meditation), being clear about what you are letting go of so you can return to secure emotional presence. This tool works well in moments when you find yourself rushing from one thing to another, lacking presence. Notice when you are in this high frequency, which drains your tank. Find a productive activity that provides release from the stress, resetting you back into balance. R&R is a needed tool in everyone's backpack!

TOOL 9

LOVE Language Communication (Listen, Open, Validate, Expectations)

When it comes to conflict, how you communicate will either make the situation better or worse. The LOVE action plan can be used with children, partners, coworkers, and anyone in your circle. It can also be used professionally with a team as a guide for directing change or confronting problems that arise at work.

When misunderstandings occur:

- *Listen* fully, asking questions for clarity to understand.
- Be *open-minded* about another perspective, using empathy language.
- *Validate* the feelings of the other person before sharing your needs.
- State *expectations* in a loving manner, collaborating on a plan that will be monitored over a period of time

By incorporating these components, your approach will nurture collaboration and understanding. Which part of this acronym do you need to practice more? Write and post this goal in an area where you will see it often, so you will remember to practice your new way of showing love to others in your life.

TOOL 10

Sandwich Cookie Conflict Resolution

As flawed individuals, we notice negatives more than positives. Sandwich cookie intention involves beginning and ending a conversation with a positive message about intention, placing the I-statement message sandwiched in the middle. This difficult message, whether written or verbal, can be used anytime you need to verbalize a healthy boundary. It is a map that guides the energy of a difficult message to be authentic and clear. Because cookies are sweet, this tool reminds you to have a sweet tone in how you speak your truth.

The tool works like this:

- Begin with intention and gratitude (cookie)
- Share your boundaries clearly using the I-statement formula: I feel ____ when ____. I need ____. (cream)
- End your message with intention and gratitude (cookie)

For example, if I am upset with the way my partner handled a parenting moment, the cookie method looks like this:

Cookie: "I want to tell you that I think you are a great dad. I want to talk about yesterday's emotions if you are in a good mindset to do that."

Cream: "Yesterday, I was frustrated when you yelled at our daughter for crying. I need you to be more patient in these situations so that she is not afraid of telling you her feelings because this could impact your relationship with her in the big picture."

Cookie: "I appreciate you hearing me on this so we can be unified in what we are teaching her. I want us to work as a team."

Stating intention before and after a boundary helps to address the problem in a positive energy and with loving words. Cookies are sweet. Be authentically sweet in how you communicate, looking at the person genuinely. It makes such a difference. Choose to keep this treat in your backpack for when you need it.

The sandwich cookie philosophy can also be a new lifestyle pattern.

Begin and end your day with peaceful intention (cookies), accepting all the ups and downs that happen in between (the cream). Start each day with a clear plan, writing down how and when you will practice best-self behaviors. At the end of the day, review your day, reflecting on what you can do better tomorrow. By beginning and ending each day with this intention, you will nurture a pattern of healthy, new habits.

My backpack toolbox can help you regulate your emotions, thoughts, and habits from here forward, nurturing your absolute best self. Choose a few tools you are willing to practice each day. Put them in your backpack so that they go with you as you journey forward. I hope they make a difference in your life.

FOR YOUR BACKPACK

Regulation is about navigating back to your best self after emotionally difficult situations. When you use tools to get back on track, you develop new skills that grow your emotional intelligence and connection with others.

CARRYING OUR BACKPACKS TOGETHER

———

"If only you could sense how important you are to the lives of those you meet; how important you can be to people you may never even dream of. There is something of yourself that you leave at every meeting with another person."

—FRED ROGERS

I have had multiple clients ask me, "How can you talk about people's problems all day long? That must be so draining!" Honestly, it is energizing. I choose to see each person for the unique strengths that help them face and problem-solve their current difficulties. On the other side of struggle is clarity. The truth is that we are all carrying something that requires growth. If you are challenging yourself regularly, insecurities are a healthy part of the process.

Your resilience comes from your willingness to be open about struggles, regulating alignment from an uncomfortable emotion to peaceful acceptance. It is not the absence of problems that makes you healthy. Managing them makes you healthy. The backpack tool teaches you to be clear on what is yours and what isn't. You are capable of overcoming the hills and valleys throughout life. It's how you grow.

The focus of your mindset becomes your experience. Isn't this amazing clarity? The backpack boundaries and tools can bring appreciation for new choices you can make to live your life to the fullest, letting go of what you can't control. Take time to understand what you carry emotionally, letting go of the negativity that weighs you down. Let go of your past hurts. Resolve them by embracing what they add to your amazing journey. Choose to live in the present moment, enjoying your moments without fear or regret. Lean into your future with faith and security. By letting go of the fear of uncertainty, you walk forward knowing that everything in your past has helped you manage this hike better.

When you choose to help someone in your life, do this because they have asked for that help and show up for them without judgment. Decide not to carry their backpack anymore. Help them put it on and walk next to them, giving support through mutual listening and sharing. When you see their backpack, remind yourself that their experience and bias belong to them. What you carry belongs to you. Remember this phrase and use it wisely.

Choose to see the contents of your backpack as a gift, regardless of your past. Decide to stop complaining about what you do or don't have in it. Do not allow anyone else to carry it, or you will limit your competence. The backpack boundaries make it clear!

If you find yourself stuck in emotion, remember the backpack mindset.

Be clear about what belongs to you.

Be clear about what belongs to others.

Be clear about what belongs to God.

Trust God fully with the big-picture tapestry that works things out for your good. Everyone can carry their own load. Although we may struggle on the tough parts of the hike, we are all capable. Walk mindfully next to others supporting the work they do to figure things out, learning needed lessons along the way.

Carrying your backpack skillfully takes work. Time does not heal your wounds. Work does. Putting in the work is about accepting and operating from a place of clear and peace-driven boundaries. You can be self-aware and regulated. Choose carefully what paths you want to take and what to put in and take out of the backpack you carry. Being clear about what belongs to you helps you hike well with others.

There are many different hikers along your way. Each backpack is different, containing unique items inside. Notice each hiker as they pass by, seeing their distinctive backpack. Along the way you will connect to some and not others. Don't limit your experience by only hiking with those like you. Get curious and brave on your hike. Learn from the strengths of the different hikers on the paths around you. Be willing to share your experience with love and compassion, listening respectively to what others say from their experience. Finally, when you understand your backpack clearly, you can share the new tools you have just learned to help others carry their backpacks securely.

Carry only what belongs to you.

Clean out your backpack often, so it doesn't get too messy.

Walk next to others, without judgment or comparison. Let others carry their backpack as they choose.

Keep moving forward, noticing the beauty around you, the strength in the hike, and embracing what is uncomfortable for personal growth.

Whatever you pay attention to grows. Be clear about what you focus your energy on, especially in the storms of life that show up along the way. Life is about choice. Despite the challenges, there is beauty all around you.

Carry your backpack securely, regardless of those hiking nearby or the challenges you face in carrying your load. Know that I will continue to carry mine with that same determination and commitment.

Oh, what joy is before us knowing we carry our backpacks together!

Never give up. Just keep going.

Carry on, carry on.

FOR YOUR BACKPACK

We are all on this hike together. No one is better or worse; each of us carries different items in our backpacks. Notice and appreciate the journey, walking next to others and securely carrying your backpack. Backpack boundaries and tools help you enjoy it even more!

ACKNOWLEDGMENTS

I have wanted to write this book for decades. I have carried many skills, tools, and stories around in my backpack throughout my career as a clinician. I have loved the process of helping people, listening to their experiences, and finding truths in what their narratives taught them. It is an honor to walk next to so many who have trusted me in guiding their healing. My clients inspired me to be my best self, working hard on their behalf. I hope that I have taught them how to celebrate all pieces of their story, nurturing a lifetime of emotional development.

As a seeker of wisdom, I honor all the amazing researchers, historians, authors, innovators, and speakers who have contributed to how I see and carry my backpack. My perspective has developed from their amazing work. Brave warriors like Brené Brown, Melody Beattie, John and Julie Gottman, Joyce Meyer, Martin Seligman, Steven Pressfield, Dr. Phil, David Eagleman, Steven Covey, Andy Andrews, Daniel Goleman, Simon Sinek, Shawn Achor, Rachel Hollis, Jay Shetty, Ed Mylett, people at the Arbinger Institute, and so many others. It is through their research and literary genius that I have created a foundation from which I have developed a philosophy of change, which I believe works on both the micro and macro level. I have seen it impact individuals and families in a profound way.

People who are intentionally congruent (aligned) with their core values, particularly in the emotionally challenged moments of life, do not fear pain or discomfort, but instead recognize the greater purpose of developing wisdom and emotional security.

Thank you, Tim Schmidt, my dear friend, for believing in me. When our paths crossed for the first time, I had no idea the impact you would have on my life. Working alongside you has taught me endless truths I didn't realize I needed to learn. You have led me to execute quickly and accept failure as learning. For this and so much more, I respect you wholeheartedly.

Thank you to Laurie Arendt, who taught me so much about the art of writing. You are a true gift, and I am thankful to have met and learned from you. Your coaching inspired and developed new skills that I now carry in my backpack.

Thank you to my Delta Defense team. I get to go to work every day with amazing people in the best organizational culture. You accepted me into your creative world from day one and it is an honor to serve you. I love all of you, dearly. You make work fun!

Thank you to the Arbinger Institute for all you do to bring well-being to workplaces all over the globe. A special thank-you to Jacob Ferrell for your support and advocacy.

Thank you to my psychotherapy colleagues (you know who you are) who have inspired and walked next to me as servant leaders. You have encouraged me, challenged me to be better, and stayed by my side throughout this process. Sara Zingsheim, you encapsulate what it means to be a servant leader. I am so grateful for all your giving!

Thank you to my parents who loved and cared for me. I know life was not always easy, but we were rich in faith and had the desire to help others. You have led me to the most important gift a parent can give: love for my Savior. Despite differences in how we live, I know you worked hard to give me what I needed to live my life to the fullest. I appreciate all you have done for me and our family. To my brother and sisters, who walk all different paths in life, carry your backpacks securely. I love you.

Thank you to my oldest sister, Amy. You had such an impact on my emotional life, being one of my greatest protectors and teachers. You have a heart of gold and your dedication to Christ's ministry is so obvious in all that you do for others. Thank you for being my memory when I needed it. You hold a deep place in my heart.

Thank you to my dear friends Krista, Carol, Lori, and Mary. We have a friendship that will forever inspire me. We are lifetime friends, carrying our backpacks side by side. I love that you encourage my shenanigans, loving me unconditionally through tough times. You are responsible for literally pushing me into the arms of the man I would end up marrying, which brought me so much joy. Little did I know that the day you shoved me into his locker would be a defining moment of my life. It set off a never-ending love story that energized my life. You are my "inner circle" support. No matter what, we support each other and will see each other through the unexpected.

Thank you for my hiking Sistas for pushing me in getting this done and for making me exercise. You brought wellness to my life without knowing it. I look up to you all!

Thank you, Schnestons, for being my tribe. I love you from the depths of my core.

Thank you to my husband and children for being with me every step of this journey. I am sure I drove you all crazy with my technology issues, writing growing pains, and my obsession to get this work into print. Todd, you have been a rock (which is not unusual). You sacrificed a great deal to support me in this process, not knowing how or if it would come to fruition. Thank you for loving me through it and standing securely by my side. You are the definition of what it means to be a partner. We have walked this life together since adolescence and I pray that we get many more decades together enjoying our love, our family, and our walk with God together.

Thank you to my daughters, Jordan, Sydney, and Payton. I hope you know deeply that although my work has been extremely important to me, it has never been as important as you. Each of you is uniquely yourself and I love being around you. When I see you, I know that God has blessed my life beyond measure. Be proud of the backpack you carry. Take time to understand it. Be accountable for your mistakes. Make the lives of those around you better by being lights. Walk closely with God because your life is not about this world. Don't get too caught up in all the drama that this material world brings. I pray that some of the things I have taught you inspire you to serve and love others to your fullest.

And as for Aaron and Kyle, thank you for the motivational conversations and for bringing new experiences to our family. Carry your backpacks securely, being leaders in every role you are given. Thank you for letting me be a teacher of your backpacks!

Thank you, Enya, for your beautiful voice that accompanied endless hours of writing. Your music kept me going. I am forever grateful.

And finally, thank you to my top-notch Scribe Media team for all the guidance and support given to make this book possible.

RECOMMENDED READING LIST

Achor, Shawn, *The Happiness Advantage: The Seven Principles of Positive Psychology That Fuel Success and Performance at Work* (Crown Publishing Group)

Arbinger Institute, *The Anatomy of Peace: Resolving the Heart of Conflict* (Berrett-Koehler Publishers)

Arbinger Institute, *Leadership and Self Destruction: Getting Out of the Box* (Berrett-Koehler Publishers)

Arbinger Institute, *The Outward Mindset: Seeing Beyond Ourselves* (Berrett-Koehler Publishers)

Beattie, Melody, *Codependent No More: How to Stop Controlling Others and Start Caring for Yourself* (Simon & Schuster)

Brown, Brené, *Dare to Lead: Brave Work. Tough Conversations. Whole Hearts.* (Penguin Random House)

Brown, Brené, *The Gifts of Imperfection: Let Go of Who You*

Think You're Supposed to Be and Embrace Who You Are (Hazelden Publishing)

Brown, Brené, *Rising Strong: Who the Ability to Reset Transforms the Way We Live, Love, Parent, and Lead* (Penguin Random House)

Burns, David, *Feeling Good: The New Mood Therapy* (William Morrow and Company)

Byrne, Rhonda, *The Secret* (Atria Publishing Group)

Cain, Susan, *Quiet: The Power of Introverts in a World That Can't Stop Talking* (Broadway Books)

Carnegie, Dale *Listen!: The Art of Effective Communication* (Gildan Media, LLC)

Chapman, Gary, *The 5 Love Languages: The Secret to Love that Lasts* (Northfield Publishing)

Covey, Steven, *The 7 Habits of Highly Effective People* (Simon & Schuster)

Cloud, Henry and Townsend, John, *Boundaries: Then to Say Yes, How to Say No to Take Control of Your Life* (Zondervan)

Gladwell, Malcolm, *Blink: The Power of Thinking without Thinking* (Back Bay Books)

Gladwell, Malcolm, *Talking to Strangers: What We Should Know About the People We Don't Know* (Back Bay Books)

Gottman, John, *The Seven Principles for Making Marriage Work: A Practical Guide from the Country's Foremost Relationship Expert* (Three Rivers Press)

Hollis, Rachel, *Girl, Go Wash Your Face: Stop Believing the Lies About Who You Are So You Can Become Who You Were Meant to Be* (Thomas Nelson)

Linehan, Marsha, *Building a Life Worth Living: A Memoir* (Random House); *DBT Skills Training Handout and Worksheets* (The Guilford Press)

Maxwell, John, *Failing Forward: Turning Mistakes Into Stepping Stones for Success* (Thomas Nelson)

Maxwell, John, *Becoming A Person of Influence: How to Positively Impact the Lives of Others* (HarperCollins Leadership)

McGraw, Phil, *Self Matters: Creating Your Life from the Inside Out* (Free Press)

Meyer, Joyce, *Battlefield of the Mind: Winning the Battle in your Mind* (Warner Faith)

Meyer, Joyce, *Approval Addiction: Overcoming Your Need to Please Everyone* (Warner Faith)

Patterson, Kelly, J. Grenny, R. McMillan, A. Switzler, *Crucial Conversations Tools for Talking When Stakes Are High* (McGraw-Hill)

Pileggi Pawleski, Suzann, and James O Pawleski, *Happy Together: Using the Science of Positive Psychology to Build Love That Lasts* (Tarcher Perigee)

Peale, Norman Vincent, *The Power of Positive Thinking* (Prentice Hall)

Pressfield, Steven, *The War of Art: Break Through the Blocks and Win Your Inner Creative Battles* (Rugged Land)

Robbins, Mel, *The 5 Second Rule: Transform your Life, Work, and Confidence with Everyday Courage* (Savior Republic)

Robbins, Tony, *Unshakeable: Your Financial Freedom Playbook* (Peter Mallouk)

Sandberg, Sheryl, *Lean In: Woman, Work, and the Will to Lead* (Knopf)

Seligman, Martin, *Flourish (A Visionary New Understanding of Happiness and Well-Being)* (Simon & Schuster)

Sharma, Robin, and Adam Verner, et al, *The Greatness Guide: 101 Lessons for Making What's Good at Work and in Life Even Better* (HighBridge)

Siegel, Daniel, *Mindsight: The New Science of Personal Transformation* (Random House)

Sinek, Simon, *Start with Why; How Great Leaders Inspire Everyone to Take Action* (Portfolio)

Sinek, Simon, *Leaders Eat Last: Why Some Teams Pull Together and Others Don't* (Penguin)

Shetty, Jay, *Think Like A Monk: Train Your Mind for Peace and Purpose Every Day* (Simon & Schuster)

Tolle, Eckert, *The Power of Now: A Guide to Spiritual Enlightenment* (Namaste Publishing)

Warren, Rick, *The Purpose Driven Life: What on Earth Am I Here For?* (Zondervan)

Made in the USA
Monee, IL
28 May 2024

59034603R00125